E ECONOMIC AND SOCIAL RESEARCH INSTITUTE

The mic and Social Research Institute (ESRI) is a non-profit orga which was founded in 1960 as The Economic Research Insti e Institute is a private company, limited by guarantee, and enjo academic independence. It is governed by a Council cons f 32 members who are representative of business, trade unio rnment departments, state agencies, universities and other resea tutes.

GENDER AND SUBJECT CHOICE

Take-up of Technological Subjects in Second-Level Education

Merike Darmody and *Emer Smyth*

The Liffey Press
in association with
The Economic and Social Research Institute

Published by
The Liffey Press
Ashbrook House
10 Main Street, Raheny,
Dublin 5, Ireland
www.theliffeypress.com

© 2005 Economic and Social Research Institute

A catalogue record of this book is
available from the British Library.

ISBN 1-904148-84-0

Printed in Spain by Graficas Cems

CONTENTS

ACKNOWLEDGEMENTS

This study was funded by the Gender Equality Unit of the Department of Education and Science. We are very grateful to Rhona McSweeney and her colleagues for their support and advice. We would also like to thank Aidan Farrell and Tony Dolan of the State Examinations Commission for providing the examination data used in the study.

We are extremely grateful for the co-operation given by the twelve case-study schools included in the study. Principals, deputy principals, guidance counsellors, teachers and students generously gave of their time and their help is much appreciated.

The study owes much to helpful comments on an earlier draft given by our colleagues, Helen Russell, Selina McCoy, Philip O'Connell, Delma Byrne and Brendan Whelan.

Chapter One

INTRODUCTION AND METHODOLOGY

1.1 INTRODUCTION

There are persistent gender differences in the take-up of subjects within second-level education in Ireland, particularly in the take-up of subjects with a more technological orientation. Previous research has indicated that technological subjects can provide a path to achievement for less academically oriented boys and a route into apprenticeships and skilled manual occupations (Hannan, Ó Riain, 1993). However, gender segregation in subject take-up means that these routes remain more or less closed to girls. This study sets out to examine the role of school provision, school policy and student choice in shaping gender differences in the take-up of the traditionally "male" technological subjects, namely Materials Technology (Wood), Metalwork and Technical Graphics. Given the importance of subject choice at junior cycle in shaping subsequent educational pathways, the focus of the study is on the take-up of Junior Certificate subjects.

1.2 Gender Differences in Subject Take-up at Junior Cycle

Students typically take ten examination subjects for the Junior Certificate; 57 per cent of students who took the exam in 2003 sat ten subjects with a fifth sitting 11 subjects. English, Maths, Irish and Civic, Social and Political Education (CSPE) are taken by almost all students with the vast majority also taking History, Geography and Science (Table 1.1). The proportion taking the other subjects reflects variation across schools in the subjects they provide, the subjects made compulsory in particular schools and the choices students make in relation to their "optional" subjects.

Clear gender differences are evident in patterns of subject take-up at Junior Certificate level. Table 1.1 shows the ratio of the proportion of female students to the proportion of male students taking each subject; a value of 1 indicates no gender differences, a value of more than 1 indicates an over-representation of female students while a value of less than 1 indicates an over-representation of male students. In keeping with their almost universal take-up, there are no gender differences in the take-up of English, Maths and CSPE. However, in spite of their high take-up rates among both girls and boys, female students are somewhat more likely to take History, Geography and Irish than their male counterparts. Clearer gender differences are apparent in relation to the other subject groupings. Female students are over-represented among those taking languages, although the disparity by gender is somewhat less marked for German than for French and Spanish. Female students are also somewhat over-represented among those taking Business Studies and Religious Education (RE)[1] and under-represented among those taking Science. The so-called "accomplishment" subjects (see Hannan et al., 1983), Art and Music, are highly gendered; female students are 1.6 times more likely to take Art than their male counterparts and 3.4 times more likely to take Music.

The most marked gender differentiation, however, is found in the technological subjects and Home Economics. Female students are almost 7.5 times more likely than male students to take Home Economics. On the other hand, male students are more than 7 times as likely as female students to take Technical Graphics and Materials Technology (Wood) and 10 times more likely to take Metalwork. Gender differences are notable, but less accentuated, in take-up patterns for Technology; however, it is worth remarking that Technology is taken by a relatively small proportion of the student cohort, indicating the small number of all schools (18%) providing the subject.

---

[1] The figures for RE should be interpreted with some caution as it was an exam subject on a pilot basis only during this period. As a result, the patterns will reflect the type of schools opting to provide the subject as well as student decision-making.

Table 1.1: Subject take-up at Junior Certificate level by gender

Subject	Male (%)	Female (%)	Female/male ratio
"Core" humanities:			
Irish	91.8	93.8	1.02
English	99.5	99.4	1.00
Maths	99.5	99.3	1.00
History	89.9	93.2	1.04
Geography	91.0	93.5	1.03
CSPE	98.4	98.6	1.00
Languages:			
French	61.8	72.8	1.18
German	18.9	20.1	1.06
Spanish	3.5	5.6	1.60
"Accomplishment":			
Art	28.4	44.8	1.58
Music	6.6	22.4	3.39
Science/Technology:			
Science	89.9	81.8	0.91
Technical Graphics	40.4	5.5	0.14
Materials Technology (Wood)	47.4	6.7	0.14
Metalwork	25.8	2.5	0.10
Technology	8.0	3.0	0.38
Other:			
Business Studies	58.6	69.5	1.19
Home Economics	8.2	60.9	7.43
RE	8.8	11.2	1.27

Note: Table excludes subjects taken by less than one per cent of the cohort.

Source: State Examinations Commission database, 2003.

What is remarkable about the patterns of take-up evident in the 2003 Junior Certificate exam is the way in which they echo gender differences evident two decades ago in the Intermediate Certificate exam. In 1980, male students were over-represented in Science and the technological subjects while female students were over-represented in the languages,

Commerce, Art, Music and Home Economics (see Hannan et al., 1983). It is worth noting, however, that there has been a shift towards less gender differentiation in relation to many of the subjects; Science has become less male-dominated while Home Economics has become less female-dominated over time. The technological subjects have also increased their representation of female students, albeit from a very low base; in 1980, male students were 160 times as likely as female students to take Mechanical Drawing (Hannan et al., 1983).

The junior cycle represents the first point within the educational system at which students can select the type of subjects they would like to take.[2] In many ways, the choices they make at this stage of their schooling career can shape their subsequent trajectories, with many junior cycle subjects acting as a "gateway" to related subjects at Leaving Certificate level. As a result, there are certain similarities between patterns of take-up by gender at junior and senior cycle. Languages remain female-dominated as do Art, Music and Home Economics. Variation is more apparent as some subjects, such as Science, become differentiated at senior cycle; Biology is female-dominated while Physics is male-dominated. The technological subjects are highly male-dominated at Leaving Certificate level, even more so than at junior cycle (Table 1.2).

In sum, clear gender differentiation is evident in the take-up of subjects at both junior and senior cycles. This variation is particularly marked in relation to the technological subjects along with Home Economics. For this reason, factors shaping the take-up of the traditionally "male" technological subjects form the focus of this study, contrasting these patterns with those for Home Economics where appropriate. Because of the small number of schools providing Technology, this subject is not a focus of this study. The following section considers the rationale for concentrating on these subjects from a policy perspective.

---

[2] A caveat is that a small minority (4%) of schools do not allow their students a choice of subjects for the Junior Certificate exam. These tend to be very small schools (Smyth et al., 2004).

Table 1.2: Subject take-up at Leaving Certificate level by gender

Subject	Male (%)	Female (%)	Female/male ratio
Humanities:			
History	24.9	17.5	0.70
Geography	58.1	47.2	0.81
Classical Studies	1.8	1.3	0.72
Languages:			
French	49.3	65.5	1.33
German	13.8	16.9	1.23
Spanish	2.1	3.4	1.61
"Accomplishment":			
Art	13.2	21.4	1.62
Music	3.3	10.4	3.14
Science:			
Physics	24.7	7.4	0.30
Chemistry	11.5	12.3	1.07
Biology	26.6	52.9	1.98
Physics-Chemistry	2.3	1.0	0.44
Agricultural Science	8.3	2.5	0.30
Technology:			
Technical Drawing	22.6	1.3	0.06
Engineering	17.7	0.8	0.04
Construction Studies	31.0	1.9	0.06
Home Economics (S&S)	9.2	53.1	5.78
Business:			
Business Studies	39.3	44.1	1.12
Accounting	11.8	12.0	1.01
Economics	11.4	6.0	0.53

Note: Table excludes subjects taken by less than one per cent of the cohort.

Source: Department of Education and Science, *Statistical Report 2002/2003*.

1.3 WHY DO GENDER DIFFERENCES IN SUBJECT CHOICE MATTER? RATIONALE FOR THE STUDY

Issues relating to gender equality have been prominent in educational research and policy discussions. Studies from the 1970s onwards documented differences in the amount of teacher time and attention given to female and male students and analysed female underperformance in the traditionally male domains of mathematics and science among other issues (see, for example, Spender, 1980). From the 1990s, a focus on the factors influencing male underperformance in examinations has come increasingly to the fore, especially in the British context (see, for example, Epstein et al., 1998). The persistence of gender differentiation in subject choices within secondary and tertiary education across a range of national contexts has meant that this issue has remained a subject for research interest and policy concern. The following section discusses some of the research conducted on the factors influencing (gender differences in) subject choice while this section provides a rationale for policy attention to gender differences in subject take-up within the junior cycle, particularly in relation to the traditionally male technological subjects.

The case for promoting equal opportunities for female and male students in access to the technological subjects centres on three main arguments. Firstly, it is important that students are enabled to develop a range of different skills as part of a holistic education. The aim of the junior cycle is to provide a broad and balanced programme of study across a wide range of curriculum areas, with science and technology as one of the eight areas of knowledge to which students should have access (NCCA, 1999). The NCCA review of technological education stated that:

> The value of technology education comes from the use of the wide variety of abilities required to produce a drawing or make an artefact, leading to a sense of competence and a feeling of personal empowerment. The acquisition of manipulative skills is an important component of this sense of competence and can help give students a feeling of control of their physical environment. In a rapidly changing global society, students need to appreciate that technological capability is necessary and relevant for all aspects of living and working (2004, p. 7).

Such skills are potentially central not only to the traditionally male craft areas with which are they commonly identified but also to a wider range of practical and design-based activities. If students do not have access to technological subjects, they therefore may lack the opportunity to develop the relevant skills for later life.

Secondly, not taking certain subjects at junior cycle level may mean that some students cannot access associated routes within senior cycle, further education/training and the labour market. Taking certain subjects at junior cycle may channel students towards related subjects at senior cycle because of the interests and skills developed by students or because of prerequisites for access to certain subjects set by schools. As a result, there is a strong relationship between subject take-up for the Junior Cert and the selection of cognate subjects at Leaving Cert level (Millar and Kelly, 1999; Figure 1.1).[3] Given the current take-up patterns, this is likely to impact disproportionately on the likelihood of female students taking technological subjects at senior cycle. Indeed, greater gender equality in the take-up of technological subjects at junior cycle appears to be a necessary, but not a sufficient, condition for less differentiation within the senior cycle since even those girls who have taken technological subjects at an earlier stage are more likely than their male counterparts to discontinue such subjects in the senior cycle (Millar and Kelly, 1999).

Subject take-up at junior cycle also has profound implications for the type of further education and training taken by young people as well as for their subsequent career pathways. Students who have taken two or more vocational/technological subjects have been found to be over-represented among young people entering apprenticeships (Hannan et al., 1998). Not studying technological subjects at school may, therefore, play some part in explaining the very low take-up of apprenticeships among young women in Ireland. Figure 1.2 indicates the number of young women and men who have received a National Craft Certificate on completion of an apprenticeship in recent years. The number of young

---

[3] This is not to imply that students do not take subjects on an *ab initio* basis at senior cycle level; a quarter of those taking Construction Studies and Engineering for the Leaving Cert had not studied related subjects at Junior Cert level (Millar and Kelly, 1999).

women involved has remained relatively stable at 20-25 per annum, with
women making up just 0.5 per cent of qualifying apprentices in 2004.

**Figure 1.1: *Proportion of students taking technological subjects at
Junior Cert transferring to related Leaving Cert subjects***

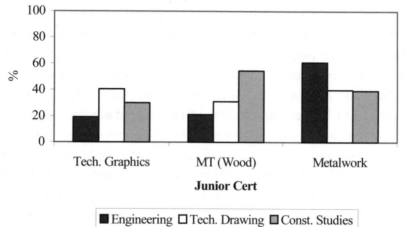

Source: Calculated from Millar and Kelly (1999).

**Figure 1.2: *Apprentices who received a National Craft Certificate by
gender 2000-2004***

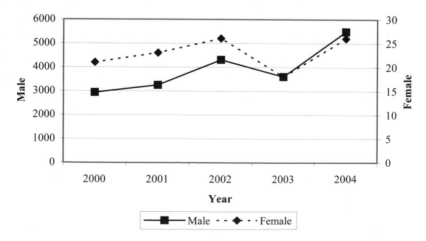

Note: Male and female numbers are presented on separate axes due to the huge disparity
in numbers involved.

Source: FÁS special tabulations.

As well as being associated with apprenticeship entry, taking more "vocational-technical" subjects is found to be associated with less time spent unemployed in the early labour market career and access to more skilled manual work (Hannan, Ó Riain, 1993). However, access to skilled manual employment is highly gendered among both young and adult workers. Women made up 3.9 per cent of skilled (maintenance) workers in 2000 and 12.8 per cent of other skilled workers, in contrast to their over-representation in personal service, clerical, associate professional and sales work. Among all women, 3.6 per cent worked in skilled manual categories compared with 21.7 per cent of men (Sexton et al., 2002). In particular craft occupations (such as carpenters and electricians), female representation is even lower, with women making up under 3 per cent of all those working as electricians, carpenters and welders (Table 1.3). Lack of female participation in craft occupations can be seen as both cause and consequence of low take-up of technological subjects at school level. Young women are less likely to take subjects such as Metalwork if they are seen as directly relating to an occupational sphere they are unlikely to enter. Similarly, they are less likely to consider such occupations if they have not developed the relevant interests and skills while at school.[4] While technological subjects may be seen in terms of orienting students towards skilled manual work, an issue which is explored in interviews with students for this study, recent changes in the syllabus of the subjects may enhance their relevance for other subject areas. This is confirmed by findings which indicate a relationship between taking technological subjects at school level and entry to third-level courses such as engineering and architecture (Smyth and Hannan, 2002; Smyth et al., 2004).

---

[4] A concern with female under-representation in these areas cannot, however, be justified in terms of potential labour shortages. The number of skilled workers (maintenance) is projected to increase by 17 per cent, and the number of other skilled workers by 19 per cent, between 2000 and 2015. This is below the average projected employment growth but is notably higher than projected increases in the traditionally female area of clerical work.

Table 1.3: Proportion female within selected craft occupations, 2002

Occupation	Proportion female
Electricians and electrical maintenance fitters	1.01
Metal working production and maintenance fitters	1.64
Welders and steel erectors	1.07
Motor mechanics	0.69
Cabinet makers	2.29
Carpenters and joiners	0.25
Painters and decorators	2.62

Source: Census of Population, 2002.

A third argument for policy attention to the under-representation of female students in the technological subjects centres on the possibility of these subjects acting as a "route to success" for students who are less academically inclined. At junior cycle, subjects with a more practical orientation, including Materials Technology (Wood), have been found to be more popular with students than some of the traditionally "academic" subjects (Smyth et al., 2004). Among school-leavers, those who had "specialised" in technological/vocational subjects were more satisfied in hindsight with the overall adequacy of their education and its contribution to their working life and personal/social development (Hannan and Shortall, 1991). Furthermore, Hannan et al. (1996) suggest that being able to take a number of technological subjects contributes to academic performance among boys in the vocational sector. Thus, being able to take technological subjects appears to enhance student engagement, retention and performance. At present, however, there are fewer subjects available for more practically oriented female students, the exception being Home Economics. This may mean that some groups of female students are not taking subjects that match their abilities and interests.

In sum, female under-representation in technological subjects is a matter for policy attention for three main reasons: firstly, because female students may lose out on developing manipulative and design skills by not taking these subjects; secondly, because the take-up patterns reflect and reinforce wider patterns of labour market segregation; and thirdly, because of the possible consequences for student engagement, retention and performance. As well as being of interest in itself, analysing the patterns shaping the take-up of Technical Graphics, Materials Technology (Wood) and Metalwork will provide an insight into the processes influencing subject choice more generally.

1.4 WHY DO GENDER DIFFERENCES IN SUBJECT CHOICE OCCUR? RESEARCH ON SUBJECT CHOICE

The Influence of Preferences and Expectations

Much research on subject choice has focused on the individual factors which shape educational decision-making. Theories of subject choice which focus on the individual level (such as the expectancy-value theory) view subject selection as reflecting two main factors: the extent to which the individual values different subject options, for example, in relation to longer-term career goals and also in relation to their current interests; and the extent to which the individual expects to achieve success in that subject (Eccles, 1994; Barnes et al., 1999; Stokking, 2000). Thus, a student will be more likely to take a subject they find interesting and one they perceive as useful in obtaining a job or accessing further study leading to employment. Furthermore, they will be more likely to take courses in which they expect to perform better, either on the basis of their previous performance and/or on their perceptions of their ability in a particular subject area. This framework has received a good deal of support from empirical research findings. Perceptions of subjects in terms of interest and usefulness have emerged as key factors in student choice across different national contexts (see, for example, Kelly, 1988; Nash et al., 1984; Smyth and Hannan, 2002). Similarly, students' past performance along with their perceptions of their ability in a particular subject (academic self-concept) are predictive of selecting that subject. Interestingly, self-concept in a particular subject is found to be more highly predictive of subject choice than actual school grades (Bandura et al., 2000; Marsh and Yeung, 1997).

This framework has implications for our understanding of gender differences in subject take-up since the perceived usefulness of particular subjects and a student's self-concept in a specific subject are shaped by broader socialisation processes; that is, an individual's beliefs regarding particular fields of study are related to cultural norms, experiences and aptitudes (Eccles, 1994). Socialisation is a learning process that begins shortly after a child is born. The process is continuous and involves learning the accepted forms of behaviour, norms and values that enable an individual to fully participate in society. The process involves gender role socialisation whereby girls and boys learn gender-appropriate modes of behaviour and values, a process that can result in gender stereotypes. Certain fields of knowledge can, therefore, come to be regarded as "male" or "female" (see, for example, Kelly, 1981, 1985; Manthorpe, 1982; Whitehead, 1996). Research indicates that gender stereotypes regarding subjects and occupations are evident even among young children. Interestingly, younger children have more stereotyped notions of the "appropriate" jobs for men and women than adolescents (Helwig, 1998; Miller and Budd, 1999). However, the extent to which a child's own occupational aspirations are gendered actually increases with age for boys but decreases with age for girls (Helwig, 1998). Because of socialisation into gender roles, then, gender differences in subject take-up may reflect differences between girls and boys in the extent to which they find certain subjects important, useful and/or enjoyable and the extent to which they (feel they) perform well in the subject (Eccles, 1994; Bandura et al., 2001; Jonsson, 1999).

The Role of the Labour Market and School Context

While theories such as the expectancy-value theory undoubtedly provide insights into some of the factors shaping gender differences in subject take-up, they have been criticised for ignoring the broader context within which individuals make decisions regarding their education (Laursen, 1993; Henwood, 1998). Two aspects of this broader societal context are worth discussing here: the labour market system and the school.

Occupational segregation by gender is a persisting feature of advanced industrial societies, although segregation levels have been found to vary across countries and over time (see, for example, Blackwell, 2001). Gender identities shape, and are shaped by, the occupational division of labour, with assumptions regarding the gender of job occupants often built into the labour process from the outset (Bradley, 1989; Cockburn, 1983; Scott, 1994; Rubery and Fagan, 1995). However, segregation patterns are not immutable; the late twentieth century saw significant feminisation in some professions, such as medicine. Segregation in occupational terms and segregation in terms of educational fields/ subjects must be regarded as interconnected. Countries with higher levels of educational segregation by gender tend to have higher levels of occupational segregation in the labour market (Buchmann and Charles, 1995; Smyth, 2002). Furthermore, subject choice must be regarded as influenced not only by cultural stereotypes regarding "male" and "female" jobs but by actual patterns of gender segregation within the workforce and students' expectations about what jobs will be accessible to them. Gender and social class also interact in shaping the expectations of male and female students regarding "appropriate" occupations, with working-class students limiting their aspirations to jobs which they perceive as accessible (Gaskell, 1984). Highly gendered patterns persist in the occupational aspirations of male and female students (Helwig, 1998; Miller and Budd, 1999). However, girls are found to be less stereotyped in their anticipated occupations than their male counterparts, that is, boys are less likely to select "female" jobs than girls are "male" jobs (Francis, 2002; Helwig, 1998; Miller and Budd, 1999). Recent research has also indicated some evidence that girls' occupational aspirations have become more diverse and ambitious than was previously the case (Francis, 2002; Helwig, 1998).

As well as being influenced by the labour market environment, students also select their subjects within the context of a national educational system (with countries varying in the degree and timing of subject choice) and a specific school situation. Schools and even school systems can tailor their curriculum according to the perceived interests and abilities of their students. Research in the United States has indicated that schools make assumptions about the abilities and needs of their student intake, assumptions which guide their decisions about which courses to offer (Oakes et al., 1992). Thus, students in predominantly working-class schools tend to have less access to advanced science and mathematical courses (Oakes, 1990; Spade, Columba and Vanfossen, 1997) and to foreign languages (Finn, 1998).

A similar picture is evident in the Irish context. The number of subjects provided and the nature of curricular provision vary by the gender and social class composition of the school, patterns which are likely to reinforce differentiation in educational outcomes (Hannan et al., 1983; Breen, 1986; Smyth et al., 2004). However, within these parameters, a school's own policy plays a role, with schools differing in the kinds of knowledge they deem appropriate for their students and consequently in the types of subjects they provide (Hannan et al., 1983; Breen, 1986; Smyth and Hannan, 2002). School and system policies reflect not only the perceived abilities of their students but also the gender of the student cohort. Historically in the Irish context, the domestic division of labour along with (until the 1990s) a relatively low level of female labour force participation contributed to female education being focused on domestic skills alongside "accomplishment" subjects (such as Art and Music) (Cullen, 1987; Raftery, 2001). However, social class was found to cross-cut the effects of gender with girls in more middle-class schools also having access to more "academic" subjects such as classical languages (Raftery, 2001).

Although historically girls in girls-only schools may have had less access to certain school subjects, some studies have highlighted the positive effect of single-sex education on attitudes to, and take-up of, maths and science, especially for girls (Ditchburn and Martin, 1986; Stables, 1990). However, other studies have found that coeducation has no significant effect on take-up patterns when adequate account is taken of the more selective nature of student intake into single-sex schools (Shuttleworth and Daly, 1997; Daly and Shuttleworth, 1997; Smyth and Hannan, 2002).

Schools with similar characteristics not only vary in their provision of particular subjects but also in how these subjects are made available to different ability groups and to girls and boys (see, for example, Lee and Smith, 1993; Oakes, 1990; Hannan et al., 1983). Thus, students in lower tracks in US high schools were found to have less access to advanced science and maths courses than students in advanced academic tracks (Oakes, 1990). Schools can also influence subject choice by how the subject is offered to students through, for example, the packaging of optional subjects. Kitchen (1999), for example, highlighted the way in which time-tabling requirements for Physics produced a gendered take-up in other subject areas. Similarly, Smyth and Hannan (2002) in the Irish context found that the timetabling of science subjects at Leaving Certificate level could facilitate gender differentiation in choices. As a result of these practices, schools with very similar student intakes can vary significantly in the proportion of the student cohort taking particular subjects (see for example, Smyth and Hannan, 2002; Davies et al., 2004a, 2004b).

Students are likely to be influenced not only by the way choices are structured within the school but by the school climate in terms of peer and teacher attitudes as well as access to formal guidance. Peer groups have been found to be influential, with boys' and girls' choices correlating with the choices of their same-sex classmates, but not with those of their opposite-sex classmates (Dryler, 1999). There is some evidence that female students may be more reliant on advice from teachers and guidance counsellors in making their choices than their male counterparts (Stables and Stables, 1995; Stables, 1996). However, although many students do cite teacher and peer influences, parents emerge as the main source of advice when selecting school subjects (Stables, 1996).

Research on the Take-up of Technological Subjects

Much research on female take-up of traditionally male subjects has focused on the take-up of science (particularly Physics) and advanced mathematical subjects (see, for example, Ayalon, 1995; Ditchburn and Martin, 1986; Stables, 1990; Kelly, 1981; Smyth and Hannan, 2002). In contrast, somewhat less attention has been given to the extremely low take-up rates among female students in the craft-related or technological subjects at school level with fewer empirical studies addressing the processes involved. Research indicates that, as with other subjects, technological subjects tend to be selected by students who feel they would be useful for a future job, by students who find the subjects interesting and by students who feel they are good at the particular subject (Kelly, 1988; Nash et al., 1984). Both boys and girls were attracted to technology education because they enjoyed working with their hands and liked the opportunity for independence and creativity afforded by these classes (Silverman and Pritchard, 1996). Advice from parents and teachers also played a role in influencing student choices. Female students were found to be more reliant on advice and encouragement from family and teachers in choosing practical/technological subjects (Silverman and Pritchard, 1996) as were students from working-class backgrounds and those with lower academic ability (Kelly, 1988). The way in which options were packaged was also found to be influential (Gillborn, 1990; Nash et al., 1984). Lack of information or knowledge about the nature and content of particular subjects played a role in students' decisions not to select practical/technological subjects (Silverman and Pritchard, 1996; Nash et al., 1984) and, in some instances, teachers were seen as discouraging non-gender-traditional choices on the part of students (Gillborn, 1990). Very little information is available on the influence of the timing of subject selection on student choices; however, Gillborn (1990) found that exposure to a subject was not sufficient to ensure gender equity in subject take-up as gender stereotyping persisted even though all students in the study were exposed to craft-based subjects for their first three years of secondary education.

Women in Non-traditional Careers

Some insight into the processes shaping gender differences in subject choice is also provided by research on post-school and career options. Women on non-traditional courses in technical colleges in the United States were found to have a higher perception of their ability to succeed in the training and a related job, had more knowledge in relation to non-traditional jobs and were more likely to see these jobs as accessible than those on gender-neutral or "female" courses (Read, 1994). Women on science and engineering courses in Canada saw their choices as reflecting an early interest in science along with support and encouragement from their high school teachers and parents (especially their fathers); in contrast, guidance counsellors within the school system were seen negatively (Ciccocioppo et al., 2002). A similar picture emerges from studies of female engineers who relate their career choice to their early experiences in maths/science and choices at school with some influence from subject teachers. In contrast, formal career advice was seen as unhelpful and negative about engineering (Evetts, 1993).

Studies of non-traditional careers among women have tended to focus on scientists and engineers rather than women in skilled manual occupations. However, one study (Greene and Stitt-Gohdes, 1997) found that women entering traditionally male skilled manual work were characterised by a belief that they had a natural ability or aptitude for the trade, a strong sense of self and a desire for independence. They had received support and encouragement for their work choices from family and teachers but did not see formal career counselling as a factor in their decision-making. Furthermore, McKinnon and Ahola-Sidaway (1995) identified a number of barriers to women entering non-traditional manual jobs including assumptions relating to physical strength, the design of tools and the work culture in terms of the use of language, joking and harassment along with social isolation (see also Dale et al., 2005). They contend that similar feelings of isolation and discomfort are evident in school-based settings for girls taking non-traditional subjects (see also Thurtle et al., 1998).

The Impact of Policy Intervention

Many researchers have identified issues for policy development on the basis of the empirical studies discussed in this section. Policy interventions in other countries have attempted to reduce the gender-stereotyping of particular subjects, with varying degrees of success (Kelly, 1985; ETAN Expert Working Group on Women and Science, 2000). The experience of the Girls into Science and Technology (GIST) project indicated that students in the intervention schools became less gender-stereotyped and more willing to accept women in non-traditional jobs; however, their own subject and career choices did not change substantially (Kelly, 1988). Some researchers have indicated the need for improved information for female students on the content of non-traditional subjects and the careers to which these subjects will lead (Read, 1994; McKinnon and Ahola-Sidaway, 1995; Silverman and Pritchard, 1996). However, Henwood (1998) argues that choices do not always reflect lack of information but must be seen in the context of other barriers facing female students. Many studies, therefore, recommend a multidimensional approach to subject and career guidance, including the promotion of self-esteem, support from teachers and peers, female role models and im-proved guidance (Read, 1994; McKinnon and Ahola-Sidaway, 1995; Silverman and Pritchard, 1996; Cockburn, 1987).

This study builds upon previous research on subject choice, both within Ireland and internationally, to explore the factors shaping the take-up of three traditionally male technological subjects at junior cycle level. On the basis of previous research, this study locates students' deci-sions regarding subject choice within the context of their interests and expectations in relation to school subjects, choice structures within the school and the social climate within which they make their decisions (in-cluding parents, teachers and peers). It is important in so doing not to view student choices as merely reflecting structures and to see students as actively involved in the decision-making process (see Laursen, 1993; Gaskell, 1984; Henwood, 1998). The following section describes the way in which the study was carried out.

1.5 RESEARCH QUESTIONS AND METHODOLOGY

This study seeks to address the following central research questions:

1. To what extent is gender segregation evident in the take-up of tech-nological subjects in second-level schools in Ireland?

2. Do the patterns of provision, and take-up, of traditionally male tech-nological subjects (namely, Materials Technology (Wood), Metal-work and Technical Graphics) differ by school type and other school characteristics?

3. Among schools providing these subjects, what perceptions do female (and male) students have of technological subjects?

4. What factors, including school policy and practice, can contribute to the promotion of the take-up of technological subjects among girls?

In addressing these questions, the study seeks to provide greater insight into the processes of subject choice in general.

The ideal way to investigate subject choice at Junior Cycle level would be to have detailed information on a large number of students and their school contexts at a point prior to students selecting their subjects.

This would allow us to control for student background in looking at the effects of school policy and practice on the likelihood of students, both male and female, taking particular subjects. Unfortunately, no large-scale database of this kind exists in the Irish context and the collection of such data would be complicated by the fact that schools vary considerably in the timing of selecting Junior Certificate subjects. Some schools require students to select their subjects before entry to the school while others allow students to try subjects for up to a year before making their final selection (see Smyth et al., 2004). In the absence of information on students prior to the point of choosing their Junior Certificate subjects, the approach taken here has been to use information on subject take-up patterns across all second-level schools in Ireland to select twelve case-study schools with varying levels of female take-up of the technological subjects. These twelve schools then formed the basis for a qualitative exploratory study of student experiences of subject choice. This approach allows us to explore students' own views of the potential influences on subject choice and place these views in the context of policy and practice at the school level.

The study draws on three sets of data:

- *The annual Department of Education and Science Statistical Reports*. Information from the Statistical Reports was used to examine trends in the take-up of the three technological subjects in the Junior Certificate examinations by gender since the 1980s. In addition, information on the proportion of male and female students taking these subjects at higher and ordinary levels and the grades achieved by students were explored. This information is presented in Chapters Two and Eight of the study.

- *The Junior Certificate examinations database of 2003*. The Junior Certificate examinations database provided information on the exam subjects taken and grades achieved by 58,058 students in 724 schools. Students taking the exam in "non-regular" settings (such as prisons and Youthreach centres) were excluded for the purposes of our analyses. Analysis of the Junior Certificate examinations database focused on three main topics: school provision of the technological subjects; take-up of the selected subjects; and student performance in the selected subjects. Firstly, the proportion of schools providing the technological subjects was analysed in terms of school type, school size, designated disadvantaged status and urban/rural location. Multivariate models were used to explore the simultaneous impact of these school characteristics on the chances of providing the selected subject (see Chapter Two). Secondly, the proportion of students taking the technological subjects was analysed in terms of student gender, age, school type, school size, designated disadvantaged status of the school and urban/rural location. Multilevel models were used to explore the influence of school characteristics on subject take-up, controlling for student gender and age (see Chapter Three). Thirdly, the level at which students took the subjects along with the grades they achieved in the Junior Certificate examination were analysed in terms of student gender, age, school type, school size, designated disadvantaged status and urban/rural location. Multilevel models were used to explore the relationship between school characteristics and exam performance, controlling for student gender and age (see Chapter Eight).

- *Case-studies of subject provision and take-up in twelve second-level schools*. The Junior Certificate examinations database was also analysed to identify schools with particularly high (or low) levels of take-up of the technological subjects among girls. Twelve schools were selected for further case-study analysis: four schools which did not provide any of the technological subjects,[5] four schools with relatively low take-up among female students in these subjects and four schools with relatively high take-up among female students in these subjects. The selected schools came from all sectors (secondary, vocational and community/comprehensive) and covered schools of varying sizes, both designated disadvantaged and non-disadvantaged schools and schools in urban and rural areas (see Table 1.4).

---

[5] For one of these schools (Downend), the technological subjects were subsequently added to the curriculum. Therefore, the school is treated as a "low take-up" school for the purposes of subsequent analyses because of patterns of subject take-up among girls at the time of the fieldwork.

Table 1.4: Profile of case-study schools

School Name	Provision and take-up	School characteristics
Park Lane	Non-provision	Girls' secondary, medium, DD, urban
Mountainview St.	Non-provision	Girls' secondary, large, ND, rural
Greenbank	Non-provision	Coed Secondary School, small, DD, urban
Clonmacken St.	Low take-up	Community/Comprehensive School, large, DD, urban
Oakleaf Ave.	Low take-up	Vocational, medium, ND, rural
Downend	Low take-up	Community/Comprehensive School, medium, ND, urban
Riversdale Lane	Low take-up	Vocational School, medium, ND, rural
Glenveagh Road	Low take-up in Technical Graphics and Materials Technology, medium take-up in Metalwork	Vocational School, medium, DD, rural
Longwell Green	High take-up	Vocational, medium, DD, rural
Southmead	High take-up	Community/Comprehensive School, large, DD, rural
Churchwood	High take-up	Vocational, medium, DD, rural
Oldham Way	High take-up in Technical Graphics and Materials Technology; non-provision in Metalwork	Coed Secondary School, medium, ND, rural

Note: DD= designated disadvantaged; ND= non-disadvantaged.

Fieldwork was carried out in the twelve case-study schools over the period March to May 2004. Within the schools not providing any technological

subjects, interviews were carried out with the principal, guidance counsellor and a group of students; in coeducational schools, separate group interviews were carried out with male and female students in their second year
of the junior cycle. Within the school providing the subject(s), interviews
were carried out with the principal, guidance counsellor, teachers of the
technological subjects, a group of female students taking the subject(s), a
group of female students not taking any of the three technological subjects
under study and a group of male students. In all cases, second year students were selected because they had already chosen their Junior Certificate subjects but were not yet influenced by the information on Leaving
Certificate choices available to third year students.

A total of eleven principals/deputy principals, seven guidance counsellors and nineteen teachers of Technical Graphics, Material Technology (Wood) and Metalwork were interviewed for the study. Among
school personnel, interviews explored the following topics:

- Subject provision in the school;

- Approach to subject choice within the school;

- Perceptions of the influences (school and non-school) on subject
  choice;

- Perceptions of the syllabus in the specified subjects;

- Approach to teaching the technological subjects;

- Facilities for technological subjects.

Focus group interviews were carried out with thirty different groups of
students from the case-study schools. Each group was made up of six
students on average. These interviews explored the following topics with
students:

- Influences on choice of subjects;

- Reasons for taking or not taking technological subjects;

- Perceptions of technological subjects in terms of content, difficulty
  etc.;

- Perceptions of gender differences in attitudes to the subjects, subject take-up and performance.

Interviews with the key personnel and students were conducted by one of the authors. They were recorded, transcribed and then analysed using the QSR N6 software package. This allowed for the identification of key themes emerging from the interviews.

The use of "mixed methods", combining quantitative and qualitative approaches, has become increasingly prevalent in educational research (Tashakorri and Teddlie, 2002; Gorard and Taylor, 2004) and has a number of advantages in relation to the study of subject choice processes. The use of national-level data allows us to document systematic differences between types of schools in their take-up of the three technological subjects and to identify schools that are "outliers", that is, significantly different from other schools in their take-up patterns. These "outlier" schools then form the basis for further research using qualitative methods, an approach that has previously been used in the analysis of school effects in Ireland and internationally (Sammons et al., 1997; Smyth, 1999). The resulting detailed case-studies of schools are thus "embedded" within wider national patterns of variation between schools. The qualitative methods used allow us to describe in rich detail the processes shaping subject choice within the context of specific schools, using the accounts of students themselves along with those of their teachers (see Johnson and Onwuegbuzie, 2004). The use of both quantitative and qualitative methods, therefore, allows us to overcome some of the limitations of each approach to provide a more holistic picture of the processes shaping subject choice within second-level schools.

1.6 OUTLINE OF THE STUDY

Chapter Two examines trends over time in the provision of Technical Graphics, Materials Technology (Wood) and Metalwork and explores whether levels of provision vary across different types of school context. Chapter Three presents patterns of take-up of the three technological subjects at junior cycle level by student and school characteristics. The nature of the subject choice process in the case-study schools is discussed in Chapter Four while teacher perspectives on the factors shaping gender differences in the take-up of technological subjects are presented in Chapter Five. Chapter Six outlines students' own views of the choice process and their reasons for choosing, or not choosing, technological subjects. Subject content and the approach taken to teaching the techno-logical subjects are explored in Chapter Seven while Chapter Eight looks at assessment and examination performance in the three subjects. The main findings of the study and the implications for policy development are outlined in Chapter Nine.

Chapter Two

THE PROVISION OF TECHNOLOGICAL SUBJECTS AT JUNIOR CYCLE

2.1 INTRODUCTION

This chapter explores the extent to which Technical Graphics, Materials Technology (Wood) and Metalwork are provided in different kinds of second-level schools. The first section examines trends over time in the proportion of second-level schools providing these subjects at junior cycle level. The second section looks in greater detail at provision patterns in 2003, assessing the extent to which the provision of technological subjects varies in relation to school sector, school size, designated disadvantaged status and location. The third section draws on interviews with the key personnel (principals, deputy principals, guidance counsellors and teachers of technological subjects) in the case-study schools to examine the factors underlying a school's decision (not) to provide any of the three technological subjects.

2.2 TRENDS IN THE PROVISION OF TECHNOLOGICAL SUBJECTS OVER TIME

Figure 2.1 indicates the proportion of schools providing Technical Graphics, Materials Technology (Wood) and Metalwork over the period 1982 to 2002. Of the three subjects, Technical Graphics was the most commonly provided with an increase in the proportion of schools providing the subject over the period. Materials Technology (Wood) was also provided by a majority of second-level schools with an increase in provision levels over the two decades. In contrast, Metalwork has been pro-

vided in a minority of schools, although provision levels have also increased over time.

Figure 2.1: Trends in subject provision, 1982-2002

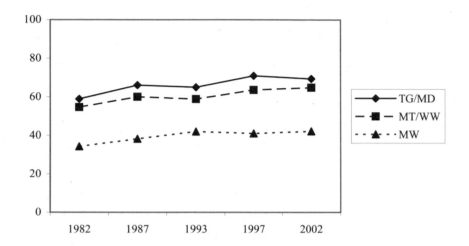

Note: The figures for 1982 and 1987 relate to Mechanical Drawing and Woodwork.

Source: Department of Education and Science, *Statistical Reports*, various years.

Figure 2.2 indicates trends in the provision of Technical Graphics over
the period 1982 to 2002. The vast majority of community/comprehensive
schools provide this subject; it is also provided in the majority of coeducational and boys' secondary schools while only a very small number of
girls' secondary schools provide Technical Graphics. The increase in
provision levels indicated in Figure 2.1 above is seen to be driven by the
increasing numbers of coeducational secondary and boys' secondary
schools which provide the subject. There has also been an increase in the
proportion of girls' secondary schools providing Technical Graphics
(from just under 1 per cent in 1982 to 8 per cent in 2002), although provision levels remain low in this sector.

Figure 2.2: Provision of Technical Graphics, 1982-2002

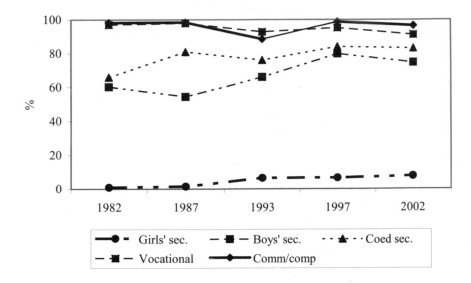

Source: Department of Education and Science, *Statistical Reports*, various years.

As with Technical Graphics, Materials Technology (Wood) is provided in the vast majority of community/comprehensive and vocational schools. By the end of the period under review, the majority of coeducational and boys' secondary schools provided the subject. Indeed, the increase in the provision levels noted in Figure 2.1 above is found to be due to increasing provision levels in boys' schools. In contrast, very few girls' schools provide Materials Technology; no such schools provided the subject in 1982, this had increased to 11 schools (7 per cent) by 1993 but decreased subsequently to 2 schools (1 per cent) by 2002.

Compared to the pattern for Technical Graphics and Materials Technology (Wood), there is a very clear distinction between secondary and other school types in provision levels for Metalwork. As with the other technological subjects, the vast majority of community/comprehensive and vocational schools provide this subject. However, only a minority of secondary schools do so and it is worth noting that no girls' secondary school has provided Metalwork over the period.

Figure 2.3: Provision of Materials Technology (Wood) 1982-2002

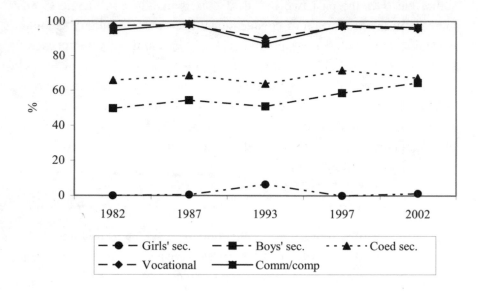

Source: Department of Education and Science, *Statistical Reports*, various years.

Figure 2.4: Provision of Metalwork 1982-2002

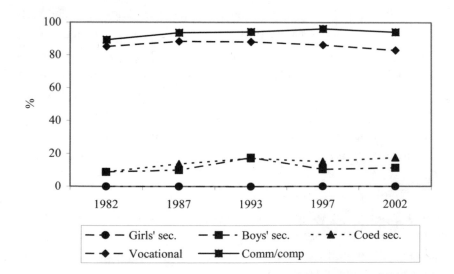

Source: Department of Education and Science, *Statistical Reports*, various years.

In sum, the provision of the three technological subjects has increased somewhat over the past two decades. This is mainly attributable to an increase in the proportion of coeducational and boys' secondary schools providing these subjects as provision levels in community/comprehensive and vocational schools are close to saturation point (except in the case of Metalwork). This section has been confined to analysing provision levels by school sector due to the lack of information on the influence of other school characteristics over time. The following section expands on these analyses by looking at the variation in subject provision across a range of dimensions.

2.3 PROVISION OF THE TECHNOLOGICAL SUBJECTS IN 2003

This section draws on analyses of the Junior Certificate Examinations Database for 2003. For the purposes of these analyses, schools are taken to provide the subject if one or more students took the subject in the 2003 Junior Certificate examination.[6] In 2003, over two-thirds (67%) of second-level schools provided Technical Graphics, 63 per cent provided Materials Technology (Wood) with Metalwork being provided by a smaller proportion of schools (41%).[7] As in the earlier period (see section 2.2), provision of all three subjects varied significantly by school type. In general, community/comprehensive schools and vocational schools tend to have much higher levels of provision than other school types, with more than four-fifths of schools in these sectors providing each of the subjects (see Figure 2.5). In addition, over four-fifths (82%) of coeducational secondary schools provide Technical Graphics. Girls' secondary schools are much less likely than other school types to provide these subjects: nine per cent provide Technical Graphics, two per cent provide Materials Technology and no girls' school provides Metalwork.

---

[6] This is consistent with the definition used for Department of Education and Science data (see Figures 2.1 to 2.4).

[7] There is a close correspondence between the proportion of schools providing these subjects and the proportion of students having access to them. Sixty-nine per cent of students were in schools providing Technical Graphics, 63 per cent were in schools providing Materials Technology (Wood) while 42 per cent were in schools which provided Metalwork.

Figure 2.5: Subject provision by school type

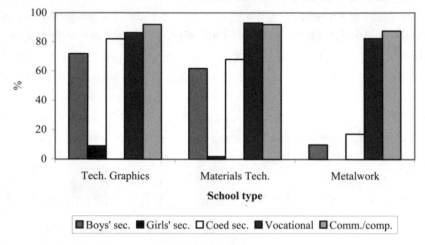

Source: Junior Certificate examinations database.

Figure 2.6: Subject provision by school size

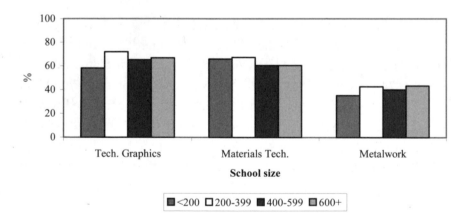

Source: Junior Certificate examinations database.

There is some variation in provision across schools of different sizes. Very small schools (that is, those with fewer than 200 students) are somewhat less likely to provide Technical Graphics and Metalwork than other schools (see Figure 2.6). In contrast, the provision of Materials

Technology (Wood) seems to be lower in larger schools (those with more than 400 students).

Figure 2.7: Subject provision by designated disadvantaged status of school

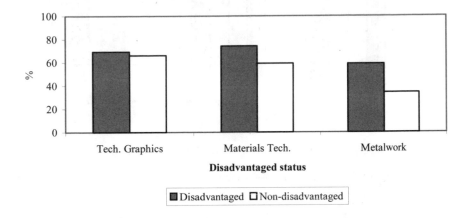

Source: Junior Certificate examinations database.

Schools which are designated disadvantaged[8] are more likely to provide technological subjects than other schools (see Figure 2.7). In the case of Materials Technology and Metalwork, this difference is statistically significant; 74 per cent of designated disadvantaged schools provide Materials Technology and 59 per cent provide Metalwork compared with 59 per cent and 34 per cent respectively of non-disadvantaged schools. Schools located in rural areas are also more likely to provide technological subjects than schools in urban areas (that is, Dublin, Cork city, Limerick city, Galway city and Waterford city) (see Figure 2.8).

---

[8] Designated disadvantaged status refers to schools receiving additional funding from the Department of Education and Science on the basis of student intake (e.g. the proportion from unemployed families). It can therefore be taken as a proxy, albeit a crude one, for the socio-economic mix of the student cohort. In 2003, 28 per cent of all second-level schools were so designated.

Figure 2.8: Subject provision by location of school

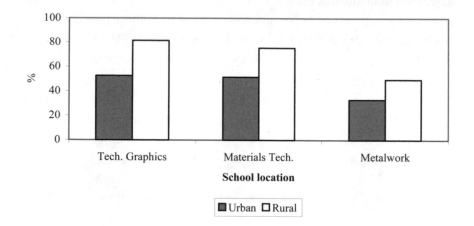

Source: Junior Certificate examinations database.

Analyses so far have examined whether levels of provision of the technological subjects vary across type, size, designated disadvantaged status
and location of school. In practice, many of these dimensions are interre-
lated; community/comprehensive schools, for example, are larger on average than other school types. A multivariate logistic regression model allows us to look at the impact of various school characteristics on the likelihood of providing the subject, all else being equal (that is, controlling for
other school characteristics). Table 2.1 presents a series of logistic regression models looking at the association between school characteristics and
the provision of Technical Graphics, Materials Technology (Wood) and
Metalwork. Positive coefficients indicate these schools are more likely to
provide the subject than the comparison group while a negative coefficient
indicates these schools are less likely to provide the subject.

In keeping with the patterns depicted in Figure 2.5, commu-
nity/comprehensive and vocational schools are more likely to provide the
technological subjects than the comparison group, boys' secondary
schools, even controlling for differences in size, disadvantaged status
and location. It is possible to convert the coefficient for commu-
nity/comprehensive schools reported in Table 2.1 into an odds ratio, re-
vealing that community/comprehensive schools are 3.7 times more likely

to provide Technical Graphics than boys' schools of similar size, designated disadvantaged status and location. Controlling for school type, school size is found to be significantly related to subject provision, with larger schools more likely to provide these subjects than very small schools. Designated disadvantaged schools are significantly more likely to provide Materials Technology and Metalwork than non-disadvantaged schools but there is no difference between designated disadvantaged and non-disadvantaged schools in relation to the level of provision for Technical Graphics. In keeping with the pattern in Figure 2.8, urban schools are much less likely to provide the technological subjects than rural schools.

Table 2.1: Models predicting provision of technological subjects (logistic regression)

	Technical Graphics	Materials Technology (Wood)	Metalwork
Intercept	0.462*	0.256	-4.058***
School type:			
Girls' secondary	-4.181***	-5.133***	-8.280
Coeducational secondary	0.257	-0.044	0.373
Vocational	0.772**	1.955***	4.383***
Community/comprehensive	1.306**	1.660***	4.131***
(Contrast: Boys' secondary)			
School size:			
200-399	1.655***	0.712	1.757***
400-599	2.011***	1.056**	2.246***
600+	2.396***	1.436**	2.923***
(Contrast: <200)			
Designated disadvantaged	-0.021	1.234***	1.099**
Urban	-2.304***	-1.920***	-1.773***
Cox & Snell R Square	0.449	0.499	0.551

Based on 724 schools

Note: *** p<.001, ** p<.01, *p<.05.

Analyses were also carried out to explore whether some schools "specialise" in the provision of the three traditionally male technological subjects. Figure 2.9 indicates that over a quarter of second-level schools do not provide any of the three technological subjects at junior cycle level. In contrast, over a third (38%) provide all three of the specified subjects. Where schools provide only one technological subject, the most common pattern is the provision of Technical Graphics. Where schools provide two technological subjects, the most frequent combination is Technical Graphics and Materials Technology (Wood).

Figure 2.9: Number of technological subjects provided by schools

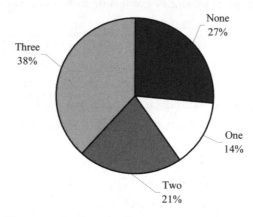

Source: Junior Certificate examinations database.

The number of technological subjects provided varies significantly by school characteristics. The majority of community/comprehensive and vocational schools provide all three technological subjects (81% and 77% respectively); in contrast, the vast majority (90%) of girls' secondary schools provide none of the three technological subjects. Designated disadvantaged schools are more likely to provide all three subjects than non-disadvantaged schools (54% compared with 33%). In addition, rural schools are much more likely than urban schools to provide all three subjects (47% compared with 20%).

An interesting contrast can be provided by looking at the provision patterns for Home Economics. Like the technological subjects, Home Economics is more commonly provided in designated disadvantaged schools (85% compared with 74% in non-disadvantaged schools) as well as rural schools (82% compared with 68% of urban schools), indicating school responsiveness to the (perceived) needs of their student cohort. In terms of variation across types of school, provision patterns are highly gendered: 97 per cent of girls' schools provide Home Economics while this is the case for only 7 per cent of boys' schools; the subject is provided by the vast majority of coeducational schools (with particularly high levels of provision in the community/comprehensive sector).

In sum, the provision of Technical Graphics, Materials Technology (Wood) and Metalwork varies significantly across different types of second-level school. These technological subjects are much more commonly provided in community/comprehensive and vocational schools along with larger schools and those in rural areas. In addition, designated disadvantaged schools are much more likely to provide Materials Technology and Metalwork than non-disadvantaged schools. The patterns of provision observed in the national population reflect a number of processes. Firstly, they are likely to reflect the impact of historical traditions in particular school sectors, particularly the traditionally "practical" orientation of the vocational sector. Secondly, they are likely to reflect assumptions about the appropriateness of certain subjects for particular groups of students with higher levels of provision in schools catering for more disadvantaged populations and much lower levels of provision in girls' schools. Thirdly, they are likely to reflect resource and size constraints with lower levels of provision in smaller schools.

2.4 FACTORS INFLUENCING THE PROVISION OF TECHNOLOGICAL SUBJECTS

Key personnel in the twelve case-study schools were asked about the factors influencing the subject mix provided within the school in general and the provision of technological subjects in particular.

The junior cycle curriculum within a school was seen to be influenced by the historical tradition and ethos of the school:

> It [subject provision] would seem to be based on what historically has worked. (Park Lane, non-provision, girls' secondary)

The availability of teachers and the qualifications of existing staff were also seen as influential in deciding the balance of subjects to be offered in the school:

> We would look at the staff that we have and look at their subjects and we would try and match that to what would have to be the basic core subjects of Irish, English and Maths and a continental language. And then after that we would look at the skills of the staff that we have because we don't have the resources to bring in extra staff for extra subjects. Because the department won't give us, won't fund us that. We would like to offer a wider syllabus but the department won't support us in that. (Greenbank School, non-provision, coed secondary)

Teacher availability was seen as a particular constraint for smaller schools:

> We're a relatively small school so I'd consult with the teachers [about subject provision]. We also take into account that we can only provide a curriculum that corresponds with the numbers we have. (Longwell Green, high take-up, vocational)

Responses in the case-study schools are consistent with patterns found in a national survey of school principals which indicated that school ethos and staff availability along with the requirements of the Department of Education and Science were very significant influences on the subjects provided at junior cycle level (Smyth et al., 2004).

A further issue relating to potential curriculum overload was raised by a number of key personnel in the case-study schools. Some staff felt that students were already taking a considerable number of, if not too many, subjects:

> I think there is more than enough even. Our big complaint here is probably that we nearly have too many subjects on offer in the school curriculum but I know looking at the exam list of subjects, I don't think we could really cram the timetable with anymore, or much more of a choice really. (Southmead, high take-up, community/comprehensive)

> The way the whole curriculum has gone in the last number of
> years they're doing an awful lot of subjects now in Junior Cert,
> like 10 and 11 subjects in some cases. And I think that's too
> broad, that they've too many things on. Because then of the num-
> ber of classes per week they mightn't be actually getting enough
> of an allocation in all the subjects to give them enough of a
> grounding in it, so sometimes I think maybe, at times I think they
> could be doing too many subjects. (Churchwood, high take-up,
> vocational)

The feeling that the junior cycle curriculum is potentially overcrowded is
likely to have implications for the ease of introducing additional subjects, such as technological subjects, into the school.

Four of the case-study schools had been selected on the basis that
they did not provide any of the three technological subjects under study
to the cohort of students who sat the Junior Certificate exam in 2003.
Two of the schools were girls' secondary schools while two were coeducational schools. In the case of one of these schools (Downend), all three
technological subjects were subsequently added to the curriculum as
school size increased. In addition, two of the case-study schools provided
Technical Graphics and Materials Technology but did not provide Metalwork.[9]

In the case of the girls' schools, not providing the technological subjects was seen in terms of the historical tradition and the stereotyping of
subjects as "male" or "female":

> I think it's based on their view of it, it's based on what histori-
> cally the view would be among all the schools in the area, that it's
> very much, Metalwork, Woodwork is a boys' thing, it's not a
> girls' thing. (Park Lane, non-provision, girls' secondary)

> I think in general it's a combination of a sort of hangover from
> tradition, from the old days.

> Interviewer: Because it's an all girls' school?

---

[9] Metalwork was subsequently added to the curriculum in one of these schools.

All girls' school and in the old days girls did certain subjects and
so on. (Mountainview St., non-provision, girls' secondary)

Similarly, key personnel in schools providing the technological subjects
mentioned the historical tradition of the school along with the socio-
economic profile of the student body:

We always had a tradition of practical subjects. It's well known
in the area. We've carried on that tradition. (Glenveagh Road,
low take-up, vocational)

They [the students] are inclined to opt for them [technological
subjects] and the school here would have a very good reputation
with regard to Woodwork and Metalwork. Students would come
to this school particularly from the national schools because we
have a very good set-up. We have good workshops and materials
and that and they know that they'll get a good grounding in those
subjects. (Churchwood, high take-up, vocational)

I suppose the tradition of the school is one of the biggest ones
[factors], that it's a long established VEC school. . . . It would
have that tradition of say practical subjects for a long, long number of years here. . . . And then they do have a lot of engineering
firms in [this town] and there would have been a link there with
them. So that would be a big thing, the whole mentality of the
town really in lots of ways was industrial in the past. (Churchwood, high take-up, vocational)

We would be relatively satisfied because as I say it's a working
class area here basically and most of the kids when they leave
here . . . the lads in particular now would be very anxious to go
into the trade. A lot of them go into the trade area of carpentry,
building, mechanics, that kind of thing. (Clonmacken St., low
take-up in TG and MT, community/comprehensive)

Non-provision of the technological subjects was also seen as reflecting
resource constraints within a school with smaller schools less available
to provide a very broad curriculum:

The size of the school doesn't allow us to have other options right now so if the school grows in the future then there will be options then to maybe offer Metalwork and that. (Oldham Way, non-provision of Metalwork, coed secondary)

Interviewer: How come this school does not provide any of the three [technological subjects]?

Respondent: For timetabling and staff reasons. We wouldn't have staff who could teach the subject and also we are offering an awful lot of subjects as it is. So there are timetable restrictions at the moment. (Mountainview St., non-provision, girls' secondary)

The cost implications of providing workshops and equipment were also mentioned as potential constraints in one of the non-provision schools as well as by staff in schools which were in a position to provide the technological subjects:

There would be things like Technical Graphics that I would have a personal interest in. I would like to see [it] on offer but obviously we don't have facilities. (Park Lane, non-provision, girls' secondary)

I don't think they [another local school] have a Metalwork workshop down there. They're expensive subjects to run to be quite honest with you, so provision for them is expensive enough. (Churchwood, high take-up, vocational)

Even the setting up of a Metalwork room or an Engineering room, it probably costs somewhere between €60,000, €70,000, whereas a normal classroom €10,000 for desks, chairs, a blackboard. So the initial set-up cost prohibits a lot of secondary schools from offering it [Metalwork]. (Churchwood, high take-up, vocational)

Personnel in the three case-study schools which did not provide any of the technological subjects felt that providing at least one of these subjects would have advantages for their students. In one of the girls' secondary schools, Technical Graphics was seen as having the potential to enhance some of the artistic subjects already provided in the school:

> I would think maybe Technical Graphics would be a very good
> one [to provide] because some of our kids would have an interest
> in graphic design and . . . art college. We would have a few for
> interior design . . . I think Technical Graphics would be very im-
> portant for them. (Park Lane, non-provision, girls' secondary)

However, a tension was evident between wanting to provide non-
traditional subjects for female students and the feeling that the demand
was not evident among the student body:

> I would like to see female students in particular having the option
> of, for example, Technology, Woodwork, Metalwork and so on,
> in the same way I'd like to see something like domestic science
> introduced in the boys' school as an option. But I don't think it
> would be very popular as an option . . . in one way I'd like to see
> it as part of the curriculum but again you can't have everything.
> (Mountainview St., non-provision, girls' secondary)

Technological subjects were also seen as potentially correcting the balance in an overly academic curriculum:

> I think maybe for the weaker student and I don't like to use that
> term but sometimes I feel that they are doing too many academic
> subjects and it would be better if they had more practical subjects.
> For example doing Technology, I think they really, really enjoy
> that, Home Economics and maybe if there was another subject
> like maybe Metalwork or Woodwork that it might be of benefit to
> them. (Mountainview St., non-provision, girls' secondary)

> I suppose in the last few years we've noticed that . . . students are
> less academic and they like to have a practical mixed in with the
> academic. And a lot of our students here, I suppose, would
> choose Home Economics because that would be the only practi-
> cal [subject] alongside Art. (Park Lane, non-provision, girls' sec-
> ondary)

In the coeducational school which was designated disadvantaged, the
lack of provision of technological subjects at junior cycle level was seen
as limiting students' options in the future, especially in the case of boys:

> I think I would like to offer certainly something like Woodwork
> or Technical Graphics, something particularly for the boys. I'm
> not saying the girls can't do Woodwork or Technical Graphics
> but we do have Home Economics, we do have Art and we have
> Science. But Technical Graphics and Woodwork is important for
> anyone who is thinking of an apprenticeship and it's a good op-
> tion to have. . . . Somebody who would have completed say
> Woodwork all the way up or Technical Graphics all the way up to
> sixth year would have a very good chance of getting an appren-
> ticeship because they would be ahead of the posse and therefore
> if we can't offer that facility, then we're at a disadvantage.
> (Greenbank, non-provision, coed secondary)

In sum, the kinds of subjects provided at junior cycle level are seen to
reflect historical tradition and ethos in conjunction with resource constraints in terms of school size and the pool of available teachers. Resource constraints in terms of providing facilities, such as workshops and
equipment, were also mentioned as influencing a school's decision regarding the provision of technological subjects.

2.5 CONCLUSIONS

The majority of second-level schools in Ireland offer Technical Graphics
and Materials Technology (Wood) to their students while Metalwork is
provided by less than half of schools. The pattern of provision is strongly
related to school characteristics with higher levels of provision in com-
munity/comprehensive and vocational schools, larger schools and those
in rural areas. Furthermore, designated disadvantaged schools are more
likely than non-disadvantaged schools to provide Materials Technology
and Metalwork.

   This variation across schools must be seen in the context of the historical traditions and student profiles across the different school sectors.
Vocational schools were explicitly established to provide a more practically and technically oriented education to their student body while
community and comprehensive schools were set up in an attempt to
bridge the gap between the secondary and vocational sectors, by providing a broad curriculum catering for pupils of different socio-economic

backgrounds and ability levels. Thus, the historical origins of these sectors are likely to have an on-going influence on the curriculum provided. Furthermore, the school sectors tend to vary in their student composition with, on average, higher proportions of middle-class students and students with higher academic abilities attending secondary schools than other school types (Hannan et al., 1996; Smyth et al., 2004). Previous research has indicated that the perceived "suitability" of subjects for particular groups of students (in terms of their ability and gender) plays a role in school policy regarding subject provision (Smyth and Hannan, 2002). These findings were echoed in the views of key personnel in the case-study schools who emphasised the role of historical tradition, school ethos and the profile of students in influencing junior cycle subject provision.

In addition, key personnel stressed the potential role of resource constraints in being able to offer technological subjects to students. Smaller schools were more limited in the number of subjects they could offer with consequent implications for the provision of technological subjects. In addition, lack of suitably qualified teachers (especially where the school has no historical tradition of providing these subjects) and the costs involved in the set-up of workshops and equipment operate as potential constraints on the introduction of technological subjects into a school.

Perhaps the most striking feature emerging from these analyses is the lack of provision of the three technological subjects in girls' secondary schools. For the Junior Certificate cohort of 2003, twelve girls' schools offered Technical Graphics, two offered Materials Technology (Wood) while none offered Metalwork. The extent to which the gendered nature of the technological subjects influences both provision and take-up levels will be explored in further detail in the remainder of the study.

The provision patterns found for Technical Graphics, Materials Technology (Wood) and Metalwork will influence the kinds of students who take these subjects. In addition, a range of factors will influence whether students choose these subjects even if they are in schools where they are provided. The following chapter will examine the characteristics of students who take the three specified subjects.

Chapter Three

THE TAKE-UP OF TECHNOLOGICAL SUBJECTS AT JUNIOR CYCLE

3.1 INTRODUCTION

This chapter examines the characteristics of students who take Technical Graphics, Materials Technology (Wood) and Metalwork for the Junior Certificate examination. The number of students who are actually exposed to these subjects will be somewhat greater due to the fact that, in some schools (those with a taster programme), students may "sample" the subjects for part or all of first year but subsequently drop the subject. In addition, some students may take a technological subject at junior cycle level but drop out of school before the Junior Certificate exam. These two groups of students cannot be examined due to the lack of available information. However, an analysis of students taking the Junior Certificate exam will provide a crucial insight into differences between students who take any of the three traditionally male technological subjects and those who do not.

This chapter distinguishes between "take-up" and "choice" of the technological subjects. "Take-up" refers to the proportion of the population of students taking the Junior Certificate exam who take the selected subject. However, as Chapter Two indicates, not all schools provide the technological subjects so it is useful to examine the proportion of students who take the subject in schools which provide the subject. This is referred to as "choice", although in practice student choice in these schools may be shaped by school restrictions on the classes and students taking particular subjects as well as on the packaging of subject choices (for example, through timetabling) (see Smyth and Hannan, 2002).

3.2 TRENDS IN THE TAKE-UP OF TECHNOLOGICAL SUBJECTS

Figure 3.1 indicates trends over time in the take-up of the three techno-logical subjects. In the early 1990s, Technical Graphics was the most popular technological subject among male students. By 2002, the take-up of Materials Technology (Wood) slightly surpassed the level of Techni-cal Graphics due to both an increase in the take-up of Materials Technol-ogy (from 43% to 46%) and a decline in the take-up of Technical Graph-ics (from 55% to 42%). Metalwork was taken by fewer male students than the two other technological subjects with take-up rates declining slightly from 28 per cent in 1992 to 26 per cent in 2002.

Figure 3.1: Take-up of Technical Graphics, Materials Technology (Wood) and Metalwork for the Junior Certificate exam 1992-2002

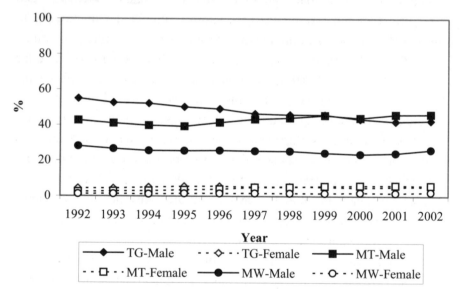

Note: This figure refers to the proportion of all Junior Certificate candidates who took each subject.

Source: Department of Education and Science, *Statistical Reports*, various years.

The take-up of the three technological subjects remained very low among female students over the period considered. There were slight increases in take-up for all three subjects: from 4.4 to 5.4 per cent for

Technical Graphics, from 2.5 to 5.9 per cent for Materials Technology (Wood) and from 1.2 to 2.3 per cent for Metalwork. Thus, by 2002 Materials Technology had become the most popular of the three technological subjects among female students, albeit at very low levels of take-up. More detailed information on the take-up of the technological subjects in 2003 will be discussed in the remainder of this chapter.

3.3 WHO TAKES TECHNICAL GRAPHICS?

In 2003, 40 per cent of all male students and 5.5 per cent of all female students took Technical Graphics in the Junior Certificate examination. Figure 3.2 indicates that students in vocational schools are more likely to take Technical Graphics than students in other school types, a pattern which holds for both male and female students. Thus, over half (53%) of boys in vocational schools take the subject compared with less than a third (31%) of boys in single-sex schools. Within all types of school, girls are much less likely to take Technical Graphics than their male counterparts. A very small proportion (1%) of girls in single-sex schools take the subject; however, in the girls' schools where the subject is provided, 12 per cent of girls take the subject. It is clear that, while gender differences in patterns of subject take-up do reflect school differences in subject provision, they mainly reflect differences among students attending the same type of school (see Hannan et al., 1983).

Students in very small schools are more likely to take Technical Graphics than students in other schools (Figure 3.3). When only schools providing the subject are considered, male "choice" patterns reflect school size with the highest rates found among students in smaller schools. Boys are more likely to take Technical Graphics than girls across all school sizes.

Figure 3.2: Take-up and choice of Technical Graphics by school type and gender

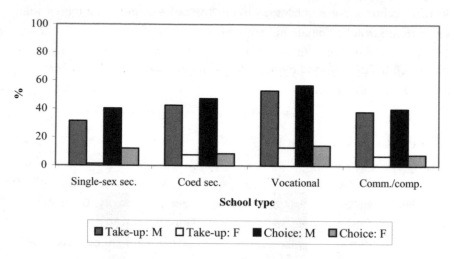

Note: "Take-up" refers to the proportion of all students taking the subject while "choice" refers to the percentage of students taking the subject among those attending schools which provide the subject.

Source: Junior Certificate examinations database.

Figure 3.3: Take-up and choice of Technical Graphics by school size and gender

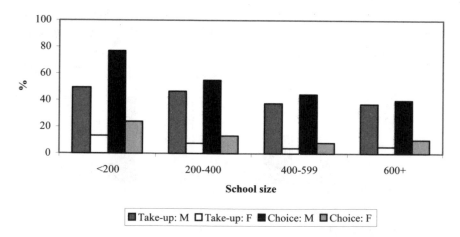

Source: Junior Certificate examinations database.

Patterns of take-up of Technical Graphics do not vary markedly by the designated disadvantaged status of the school (see Figure 3.4). Students in rural schools are much more likely to take Technical Graphics than those in urban schools (see Figure 3.5).

Figure 3.4: Take-up and choice of Technical Graphics by disadvantaged status and gender

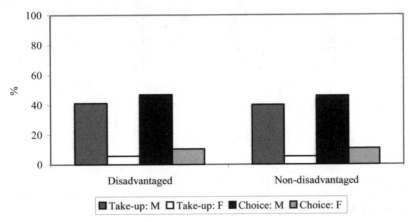

Source: Junior Certificate examinations database.

Figure 3.5: Take-up and choice of Technical Graphics by school location and gender

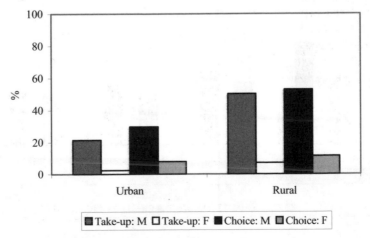

Source: Junior Certificate examinations database.

Table 3.1: Factors influencing the take-up and choice of Technical Graphics (Multilevel logistic regression)

	Subject take-up (All students)	Subject "choice" (Students in schools providing TG)
Intercept	-0.091	0.745*
Student characteristics		
Female	-2.326*	-0.558*
Age:		
15-15½	0.090	0.016*
15½-16	0.052	0.009
>16	-0.052	-0.011
(Contrast: <15)		
School characteristics		
School type:		
Boys' secondary	-0.193	-0.044
Girls' secondary	-1.756*	0.039
Vocational	0.545*	0.075*
Community/comprehensive	0.096	-0.030
(Contrast: Coed secondary)		
Vocational*female	0.271*	-0.007
Comm./comp.*female	0.013	0.015
School size:		
200-399	0.134	-0.165*
400-599	0.030	-0.248*
600+	0.044	-0.270*
(Contrast: <200)		
200-399*female	-0.152	0.061*
400-599*female	-0.327*	0.108*
600+*female	0.258	0.176*
Designated disadvantaged	-0.072	0.004
Disadvantaged*female	-0.075	-0.003
Urban	-1.533*	-0.201*
Urban*female	0.669*	0.205*
School-level variance:		
Null model	1.575*	0.040*
Controlling for student and school characteristics	4.955*	0.025*
N	58,058 students, 724 schools	40,216 students, 485 schools

Note: * p<.05.

It is possible to examine the school and student factors that influence the "take-up" and "choice" of Technical Graphics by using multilevel modelling. Multilevel modelling techniques allow us to take account of the fact that students in the same school are more likely to resemble each other since they face common school structures and processes. In Table 3.1, the first column compares students taking the subject with all students taking the Junior Cert who do not take Technical Graphics. The second column looks at the factors associated with taking the subject only among those in schools providing the subject. Positive coefficients indicate these students are more likely to take Technical Graphics than the comparison group while a negative coefficient indicates these students are less likely to take the subject.

Female students are much less likely to take Technical Graphics than male students, even controlling for school characteristics (see Table 3.1). Students taking the subject do not vary markedly in age from those not taking it; however, within schools providing the subjects, students aged 15-15½ years of age are somewhat more likely to take Technical Graphics than younger students. Controlling for student gender and age, take-up rates are highest in vocational schools and lowest in girls' secondary schools. When only "providing" schools are considered, the main distinction in "choice" levels is between vocational schools and all other school types, with students in the vocational sector more likely to select the subject. Take-up rates do not vary markedly by school size or disadvantaged status. However, within schools which provide Technical Graphics, those in very small schools are more likely to take the subject than those in larger schools. Students in urban schools are less likely to take Technical Graphics even if they are in schools providing the subject.

These models indicate that girls are much less likely than boys to take Technical Graphics at Junior Certificate level. However, they also allow us to investigate whether the gender gap varies across different types of schools by including interaction terms in our models. In terms of subject choice patterns, the gender gap is found to vary by school size and location. In other words, there is greater gender equality in choice patterns in larger schools and in urban schools. This may reflect greater gender stereotyping in schools with a more constrained curriculum since smaller schools are in a position to provide fewer subjects (Smyth et al., 2004).

Even taking into account student and school characteristics, the school-level variance term indicates that schools of similar profiles differ significantly in the proportion of their students who take Technical Graphics. Thus, certain individual schools will have higher (or lower) take-up rates than average.

3.4 WHO TAKES MATERIALS TECHNOLOGY (WOOD)?

In 2003, 47 per cent of all male students and 7 per cent of all female students took Materials Technology (Wood) in the Junior Certificate exam. Figure 3.6 indicates that students in vocational schools are more likely to take Materials Technology (Wood) than students in other school types, a pattern that holds for both male and female students. The lowest take-up rates are found in single-sex secondary schools, particularly among girls.

Figure 3.6: Take-up and choice of Materials Technology (Wood) by school type and gender

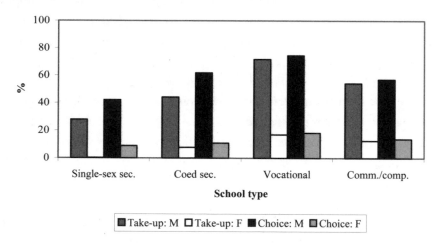

Source: Junior Certificate examinations database.

As with Technical Graphics, female students are much less likely to take Materials Technology (Wood) than male students in the same sector. Both the take-up and choice rates decline with school size, that is, students in larger schools are much less likely to select Materials Technology (Figure 3.7). Students in designated disadvantaged schools are more likely to take Materials Technology than those in non-disadvantaged schools (Figure 3.8) while those in rural schools are more likely to take the subject than those in urban schools (Figure 3.9).

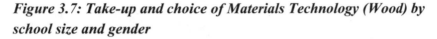

Figure 3.7: Take-up and choice of Materials Technology (Wood) by school size and gender

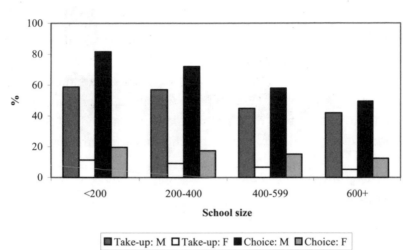

Source: Junior Certificate examinations database.

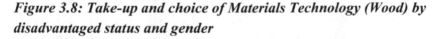

Figure 3.8: Take-up and choice of Materials Technology (Wood) by disadvantaged status and gender

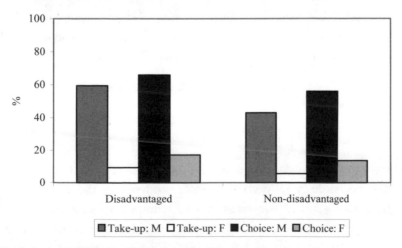

Source: Junior Certificate examinations database.

Figure 3.9: Take-up and choice of Materials Technology (Wood) by school location and gender

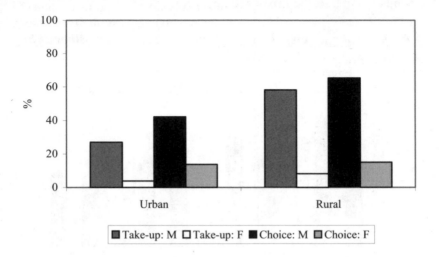

Source: Junior Certificate examinations database.

Using a multilevel logistic regression model to look at the impact of school and student characteristics simultaneously, the take-up of Materials Technology (Wood) is found to be related to student gender and age with the lowest take-up rates found among girls and younger students. Those aged over 16 years of age are 1.4 times more likely to "choose" Materials Technology than those aged under 15 years of age. This may relate to the fact that students who are significantly older than average tend to have lower levels of academic performance and may be less oriented to traditional "academic" subjects than other students (Hannan et al., 1996).

Table 3.2: Take-up and choice of Materials Technology (Wood) (Multilevel logistic regression)

	Subject take-up (All students)	Subject "choice" (Students in schools providing MT)
Intercept	-0.030	1.277*
Student characteristics		
Female	-2.668*	-3.388*
Age:		
15-15½	0.063	0.076
15½-16	0.162*	0.189*
>16	0.269*	0.311*
(Contrast: <15)		
School characteristics		
School type:		
Boys' secondary	-0.432	-0.650*
Girls' secondary	-3.504*	0.095
Vocational	1.266*	0.591*
Community/comprehensive	0.638*	-0.004
(Contrast: Coed secondary)		
Vocational*female	-0.191*	0.064
Comm./comp.*female	0.119	0.308*
School size:		
200-399	0.161	-0.412*
400-599	-0.151	-0.886*
600+	-0.421	-1.106*
(Contrast: <200)		
200-399*female	0.120	0.362*
400-599*female	0.239	0.664*
600+*female	0.246	0.724*
Designated disadvantaged	0.490*	0.285*
Disadvantaged*female	-0.235*	-0.115
Urban	-1.546*	-0.857*
Urban*female	0.972*	0.876*
School-level variance:		
Null model	1.617*	0.509*
Controlling for student and school characteristics	4.192*	0.548*
N	58,058 students, 724 schools	36,480 students, 459 schools

Note: * p<.05.

Controlling for student gender and age, take-up rates are highest in vocational schools and lowest in girls' secondary schools (Table 3.2). When
only schools providing Materials Technology are considered, students in
vocational schools are most likely to choose the subject and those in
boys' secondary schools least likely to do so. As with Technical Graphics, the proportion of students choosing the subject declines with school
size. Students in designated disadvantaged schools are more likely, and
those in urban schools less likely, to take Materials Technology (Wood).
The gender gap is somewhat reduced in community/comprehensive
schools, in larger schools and in urban schools.

Even controlling for student and school characteristics, schools vary
significantly in the proportion of students taking Materials Technology
(Wood).

3.4 WHO TAKES METALWORK?

In 2003, Metalwork had the lowest take-up among the three technological subjects with 26 per cent of all male students and 2.5 per cent of all
female students taking the subject for the Junior Certificate exam. As
with the other technological subjects, the take-up of Metalwork is highest in vocational schools and lowest in single-sex schools (Figure 3.10).
Because no girls' schools provide Metalwork (see Chapter Two), no girls
in single-sex schools can "choose" the subject. Take-up and choice rates
for Metalwork are highest in very small schools (Figure 3.11), designated disadvantaged schools (Figure 3.12) and rural schools (Figure
3.13). The exception to the latter pattern occurs for girls in schools providing Metalwork with those in urban schools more likely to choose the
subject than those in rural schools (9% compared with 6.5%).

All else being equal, female students are much less likely to take
Metalwork than male students in similar types of schools (Table 3.3).
Older students (those over 16 years of age) are most likely to take the
subject. Students in vocational schools are more likely to choose the subject than other students, as are those in very small schools. Students in
designated disadvantaged schools are more likely to take Metalwork, as
are those in rural schools. The gender gap is reduced somewhat in vocational schools compared with other school types. The gender gap is also

reduced in larger schools and in schools located in urban areas. Even controlling for student and school characteristics, second-level schools differ significantly in the proportion of their students taking Metalwork for the Junior Certificate exam.

Figure 3.10: Take-up and choice of Metalwork by school type and gender

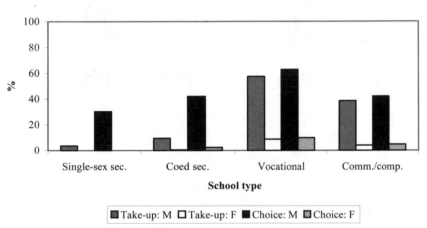
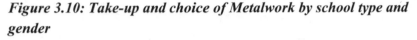

Source: Junior Certificate examinations database.

Figure 3.11: Take-up and choice of Metalwork by school size and gender

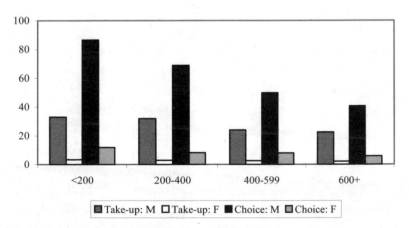

Source: Junior Certificate examinations database.

Figure 3.12: Take-up and choice of Metalwork by designated disad-vantaged status and gender

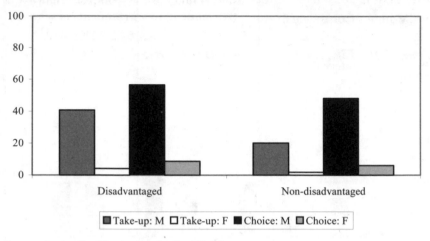

Source: Junior Certificate examinations database.

Figure 3.13: Take-up and choice of Metalwork by school location and gender

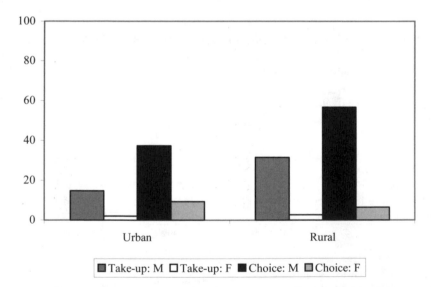

Source: Junior Certificate examinations database.

Table 3.3: Take-up and choice of Metalwork (Multilevel logistic regression)

	Subject take-up (All students)	Subject "choice" (Students in schools providing MW)
Intercept	-3.362*	1.015*
Student characteristics		
Female	-3.626*	-4.580*
Age:		
15-15½	0.130*	0.146*
15½-16	0.137*	0.155*
>16	0.276*	0.321*
(Contrast: <15)		
School characteristics		
School type:		
Boys' secondary	-0.157	-0.201
Vocational	3.284*	0.823*
Community/comprehensive	2.580*	0.226
(Contrast: Coed secondary)		
Vocational*female	1.036*	0.686*
Comm./comp.*female	0.613*	0.290
School size:		
200-399	0.394	-0.968*
400-599	0.136	-1.645*
600+	0.253	-1.865*
(Contrast: <200)		
200-399*female	-0.787*	0.350*
400-599*female	-0.212*	1.019*
600+*female	0.068	1.272*
Designated disadvantaged	0.834*	0.361*
Disadvantaged*female	0.222*	0.150
Urban	-1.113*	-0.544*
Urban*female	1.158*	1.127*
School-level variance:		
Null model	2.767*	0.621*
Controlling for student and school characteristics	6.024*	0.614*
N	58,058 students, 724 schools	24,554 students, 298 schools

Note: * p<.05. Girls' secondary schools are not included as a variable as no students in these schools took Metalwork.

3.5 SUBJECT SPECIALISATION AMONG STUDENTS

The previous sections have explored the factors influencing the take-up of the three technological subjects separately. However, it is also worth exploring whether some students "specialise" by taking a number of these subjects at junior cycle level. Figure 3.14 indicates the number of technological subjects taken by Junior Certificate students in 2003. Over half (58%) of all students take none of the three technological subjects while relatively few students (5%) "specialise" by taking all three subjects.

Figure 3.14: Number of technological subjects taken

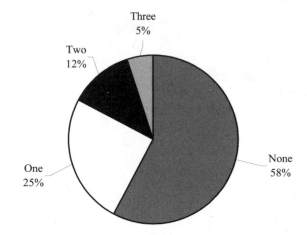

Source: Junior Certificate examinations database.

The degree of specialisation varies markedly by gender (see Figure 3.15). The vast majority (87%) of female students take none of the technological subjects while the majority (71%) of male students take at least one such subject. A tenth of male students take all three technological subjects. Among both male and female students, older students tend to take more technological subjects than younger students; 13 per cent of male students aged 16 or over take all three subjects compared with 7 per cent of those aged under 15 years of age. The degree of specialisation also varies by school type. Male students in vocational schools are the group most likely to specialise in technological subjects; 30 per cent of them take all three subjects while 33 per cent take two such subjects. Furthermore, those in small schools are most likely to specialise in technological subjects (for males, 25% compared with 5% in very large schools) as are those in designated disadvantaged schools (16% compared with 7% in non-disadvantaged schools for males) and rural schools (14% compared with 1% in urban schools for males).

Figure 3.15: Number of technological subjects taken by gender

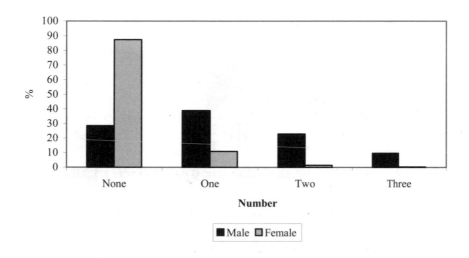

Source: Junior Certificate examinations database.

3.6 BACKGROUND DIFFERENCES IN TAKE-UP

The Junior Certificate examinations database allows us to explore the influence of some student characteristics along with school characteristics on the take-up of the three technological subjects. However, it contains only limited information on student characteristics (namely, gender and age) and does not contain information on background characteristics, such as prior "ability"/performance and parental social class, factors which have been found to be associated with the take-up of particular subjects (Hannan et al., 1983; Breen, 1986; Smyth and Hannan, 2002).

One way of looking indirectly at the profile of male and female students who take the technological subjects is to explore their performance in Junior Certificate English and Mathematics. This allows us to assess whether students taking the subjects achieve above or below average grades in the traditional "academic" subjects. It is not intended, however, to imply any causal relationship between taking technological subjects and performance in English and Maths; rather it is attempting to use performance in English and Maths as a proxy for pre-existing differences in academic "ability".

Figure 3.16: Performance "gap" in English and Mathematics between those taking technological subjects and other students by gender

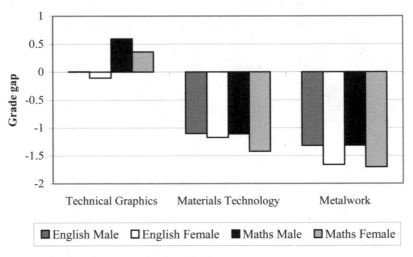

Source: Junior Certificate examinations database.

Figure 3.16 indicates the performance gap in English and Mathematics between those taking the specified technological subjects and those who do not take the subjects. Performance in English and Maths is scored from 0 (indicating a grade of "E", "F" or "NG") to 10 (indicating an "A" grade on a higher level paper) and then transformed so that zero indicates the average grade in English and Maths across all students taking the Junior Certificate in 2003. Male students who take Technical Graphics tend to achieve average grades in English but slightly above average grades in Junior Certificate Mathematics. Female students who take Technical Graphics also achieve slightly above average Maths grades but their English grades are somewhat below the national average. Students who take Materials Technology (Wood) and Metalwork tend to achieve significantly lower English and Maths grades than those who do not. The difference is greater for female than for male students. In the case of Metalwork, for example, the scale of the difference for male students is the difference between a B and a C grade in English on an ordinary level paper while for female students the difference is almost that between a B and a D grade. Thus, it appears that the take-up of Materials Technology and Metalwork is highest among students with somewhat lower levels of academic ability and that these subjects appear to attract a somewhat broader range of abilities among boys than girls. In contrast, Technical Graphics appears to attract students who are of average ability in English but slightly above average ability in Maths, perhaps reflecting the use of geometrical and other mathematical concepts in Technical Graphics.

A similar pattern is evident if alternative proxies for academic "ability", the overall Junior Certificate exam score and the number of higher level papers taken, are considered. Among male students, those who take Technical Graphics tend to achieve slightly higher average Junior Cert exam grades than those who do not take the subject; there is no significant difference in exam performance between female students who take Technical Graphics and those who do not. Both male and female students taking Materials Technology and Metalwork tend to achieve significantly lower Junior Cert exam grades than those who do not take these subjects (Figure 3.17). As with the pattern for English and Maths grades, the performance gap is greater for female students indicating that these subjects tend to attract lower-performing girls. The performance gap in the case of Materials Technology and Woodwork is around the difference between a B and a C grade on an ordinary level paper for every exam subject taken.

***Figure 3.17: Performance gap in average Junior Certificate exam
grades between those taking technological subjects and other students
by gender***

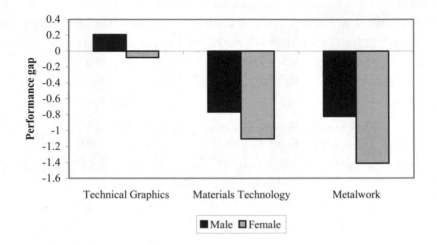

Source: Junior Certificate examinations database.

In keeping with the patterns in relation to exam grades, male students
taking Technical Graphics tend to take slightly more higher level subjects than those not taking the subject; no such difference is evident
among female students. For both Materials Technology and Metalwork,
students taking these subjects tend to take fewer higher level subjects
than those not taking the subjects (Figure 3.18). For example, girls taking Metalwork tend to take three higher level subjects on average compared with an average of six among those not taking the subject.

Figure 3.18: Average number of higher level subjects taken by take-up of technological subjects and gender

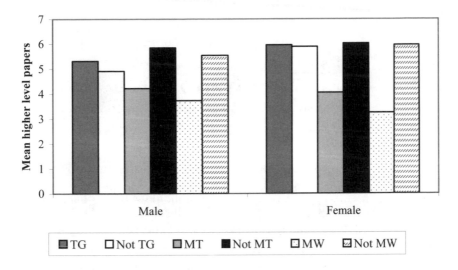

Source: Junior Certificate examinations database.

3.7 CONCLUSIONS

This chapter has indicated that students who take Technical Graphics, Materials Technology (Wood) and Metalwork differ in gender, age and school characteristics from those who do not take these subjects. These differences are not explained by differences between schools in whether they provide technological subjects or not since, even among schools providing technological subjects, certain differences are evident. Firstly, students in the vocational sector are more likely to "choose" technological subjects than those in other school types, even controlling for school size, disadvantaged status and location. Secondly, students attending smaller schools are more likely to select technological subjects than those in larger schools. Thirdly, students attending schools in the urban centres are less likely to choose technological subjects than their rural counterparts. Fourthly, students in designated disadvantaged schools are more likely to take Materials Technology (Wood) and Metalwork than those in non-disadvantaged schools.

The higher proportion of students taking technological subjects in vocational and designated disadvantaged schools must be seen in the context of the socio-economic and "ability" profile of students attending these schools. Thus, students are less likely to be oriented to traditional "academic" subjects and more likely to choose subjects with a technological orientation. Furthermore, they are more likely to come from working-class backgrounds and thus may be oriented towards (skilled) manual work in the future, seeing technological subjects as a route to this end (see Hannan, Ó Riain, 1993).

The relationship between take-up of technological subjects and school size may reflect a more constrained curriculum in smaller schools. On the one hand, smaller schools are more likely than other schools to offer students no choice of subjects at junior cycle level (Smyth et al., 2004), although the number of schools so doing are few; thus, if these schools provide technological subjects, all students in the school will take them. On the other hand, smaller schools tend to provide fewer subjects than larger schools although their students take the same number of subjects on average as students in other schools (Smyth et al., 2004). Thus, students attending smaller schools will be more constrained in their choices regarding subjects. The rural-urban difference in the proportion of students is more difficult to explain but may be related to historical tradition.

In terms of student characteristics, older students are more likely than their younger counterparts to take Materials Technology (Wood) and Metalwork. There is also tentative evidence that Technical Graphics attracts female students from a broad range of abilities and male students who are mathematically inclined. In contrast, Materials Technology (Wood) and Metalwork tend to attract students who have lower grades in the other academic subjects, a pattern which is particularly marked for girls. It should be noted, however, that information would be required on students' academic "ability" prior to entering junior cycle in order to confirm these patterns more definitively.

Chapter Two has indicated that girls are less likely to attend schools where the technological subjects are provided. However, even where girls attend schools providing these subjects, they are significantly less likely than their male counterparts to select them. It is worth noting that the gender gap is somewhat reduced in certain schools, namely, larger schools and those located in urban areas. It may be that the constrained curriculum in smaller schools tends to result in greater gender stereotyping in subject choice, for example, as a result of the packaging of subjects and time-tabling practices. Previous research (Gash et al., 1993) has indicated greater gender role stereotyping among students attending primary schools in rural areas; this may, at least in part, explain the reduced gender gap found in urban schools. It is worth noting, however, that, while girls attending larger and/or urban schools are more likely to take technological subjects *relative* to their male counterparts than those in smaller rural schools, the *absolute* number of girls taking these subjects remains fairly low and has not changed markedly in two decades.

An analysis of the examinations database allows us to identify differences between schools in the proportion of students taking Technical Graphics, Materials Technology (Wood) and Metalwork. However, it does not allow us to explain why these school differences emerge. For the purposes of this study, case-studies of schools were conducted in order to look at school organisation and process in schools with varying levels of take-up of the technological subjects (see Chapter One). The following chapter explores the choice process in the case-study schools, that is, how schools allow students to select their Junior Certificate subjects, and asks key personnel about the factors which they consider influence subject choice in general and take-up of the technological subjects in particular. Student perspectives on the choice process and the influences on subject take-up are then presented in Chapter Six.

Chapter Four

SUBJECT CHOICE IN THE CASE-STUDY SCHOOLS

4.1 INTRODUCTION

S econd-level schools vary in the approach they take to subject choice, ranging from schools who do not allow students a choice of Junior Certificate subjects to ones where students try out all of the subjects during (part or all of) first year before selecting the subjects they want to take for the Junior Certificate examination (Smyth et al., 2004). The school's approach to subject choice is likely to have implications not only for the number of subjects students will take but for the kinds of subjects which they will select. This chapter explores the approach to subject choice taken by the case-study schools, focusing in particular on the choice of the three technological subjects. The second section outlines the timing of subject choice in the case-study schools. The third section examines perceptions among key personnel of the factors influencing students' choice of Junior Certificate subjects. In the fourth section, the focus is on the choice of technological subjects and the way in which students select these subjects. The issue of gender differences in the take-up of technological subjects is discussed in greater detail in Chapter Five.

4.2 THE NATURE AND TIMING OF SUBJECT CHOICE

As is the case for second-level schools nationally, the case-study schools varied in the timing of subject choice along with their approach to ability grouping (see Table 4.1).

Table 4.1: Approach to subject choice and ability grouping

School	Subject Choice	Ability Grouping (base classes)
Non-provision		
Park Lane	Taster programme (all of first year)	Streaming/Banding
Mountainview St.	Before or on entry (had previously had a taster programme)	Mixed ability
Greenbank	Taster programme (part of first year)	Streaming/Banding
Low take-up		
Downend	Taster programme for part of first year (with some pre-selection on entry)	Mixed ability
Glenveagh Road	Before or on entry (sampling on first day); access to subjects linked to class allocation	Streaming/Banding
Clonmacken St.	Before or on entry; access to subjects linked to class allocation	Streaming/Banding
Oakleaf Ave.	Before or on entry	Streaming/Banding
Riversdale Lane	Before or on entry	Mixed ability
High take-up		
Longwell Green	Before or on entry; access to subjects linked to class allocation	Streaming/Banding
Southmead	Before or on entry; access to subjects linked to class allocation	Streaming/Banding
Churchwood	Before or on entry; access to subjects linked to class allocation	Streaming/Banding
Oldham Way	Taster programme (part of first year)	Mixed ability

Among the schools not providing the technological subjects, two schools had a taster programme, allowing students to try out subjects before making a final selection, while one school required students to pick their subjects before coming to the school. Among the nine schools providing the technological subjects, two had a taster programme while seven schools required students to select their subjects before or on entering the school. On the basis of the case-study schools, there appears to be no clear relationship between the timing of subject choice and whether female students have a higher take-up of the technological subjects.

Key personnel saw the taster programme approach as facilitating a more informed choice among students, allowing them to select Junior Certificate subjects which matched their interests and abilities:

> When they try out each of the subjects, we find that mostly it [subject choice] will come down to their aptitude for the subject and their enjoyment of the subject. (Oldham Way, high take-up, coed secondary)

> It is a good idea to do it that way [taster programme], give them a choice that way and see how they get a taste for it. Because when they come in, in first year they have a fair idea what Art is, they have no idea what Technical Graphics is, they think they know what some of the other subjects are. And when they get a taste of it, it gives them a better option. (Churchwood, high take-up, vocational)

However, a number of staff in schools without taster programmes were critical of this approach to subject choice. Firstly, a "sampling" approach was seen as creating difficulties in covering the curriculum with first year students:

> A lot of teachers felt "I have lost four months of teaching by all this sampling" because you couldn't really start the syllabus and you had to teach it in a different way. (Mountainview St., non-provision, girls' secondary)

> The reason we don't provide a taster programme is very simple: a lot of the kids we have here, their ability wouldn't be that high and they would need the full three years to be sufficient. In some

of the subjects they would take as an option, they may not handle
it in two years. That's the reason for it. (Clonmacken St., low
take-up, community/comprehensive)

It was also considered that taking a subject for a short period of time did
not necessarily give students an accurate idea of the content of that subject:

The difficulty with it is that if they're sampling everything, you
only have them for a very short period of time. And it's very difficult where they're starting something from scratch, [. . .] to get
it to a stage where you can actually motivate them. Because it's
like learning the vocabulary, you have to spend so much time at
the basics to get them up to a level where they can do the very
basic stuff. It's very hard to make Technical Graphics interesting
for them at the very beginning because they don't have the basics
of using the drawing equipment and so on; they don't have the
basic constructions that will enable them to do the stuff that gets
interesting. So it's very hard to do that in a very short space of
time. (Downend, low take-up, community/comprehensive)

Secondly, a taster approach was seen as creating logistical problems for
schools in ensuring that students could select the subjects they wanted:

We did it last year and we allowed them from September to
Christmas to sample Music, Home Economics, Science etc., etc.
They were able to sample every subject and it did not work and
we said "we will never do it again". Because when it came to
January we discovered . . . for example ninety-eight wanted to do
Music, we could only offer it to forty students; so because every-
body had sampled it they all wanted to do it. So there were a lot
of very disillusioned students and parents. So it was not a good
idea. (Mountainview St., non-provision, girls' secondary)

Thirdly, having to try all of the subjects for part or all of first year was
seen as facilitating student disaffection in cases where students disliked
particular subjects but were nevertheless required by school policy to
take them:

> Let's say we have Technical Graphics and Art and somebody is told you're doing Technical Graphics for the year for two classes and two Art classes. They don't want to be there, they don't like it, they know what they want to do before they come in, they know after the first week: "I want to do Art", "why can't I do four classes of Art", "you're forcing me to do a subject for two classes that I don't want to do and at the end of the year I'm telling you I won't be doing it", so they're frustrated and upset that they're being forced to do it. A teacher is put to the pin of their collar to try and make it interesting while a kid is sitting there saying I don't care what you do, you can have a three-ring circus in here, I don't want to be here. And everyone is going to suffer, discipline is going to be a problem then, so I think it's much easier and a fairer system [to have early choice]. (Churchwood, high take-up, vocational)

Because of the differences between the case-study schools in the timing of subject choice, schools varied in the information given to students regarding the different subjects on offer. In the case of schools with taster programmes, having the chance to "sample" the subjects was seen as providing students with a greater insight into the subject (see above). Among schools without taster programmes, two main approaches were taken to giving students information regarding their subject choices. In the first group of schools, information on the different subject options was presented as part of an open day or evening for students and their parents:

> We have a "familiarisation evening" at the end of August where the students who have enrolled in the school and their parents are invited up to the school for an evening and that's when the basic school rules, the expected behaviour, the subjects on offer, the different options that they have, that will be explained. (Churchwood, high take-up, vocational)

> The focus was on the open night to introduce all parents in the locality to what is on offer subject-wise for their children in this school and they were given plenty of information in the form of talks and handouts, so I think it was very well covered. (Oldham Way, high take-up in TG and MT, coed secondary)

In the second group of schools, a somewhat more proactive approach to the transition from primary to second-level education was taken, with school personnel visiting local primary schools and visits by primary schoolchildren to the schools:

> We . . . have an induction day for the sixth class students in our catchment schools where they are taken to the practical rooms, to the drawing rooms and where we'd speak to them. So every person that's entering the school is given an equal opportunity, they make the choice themselves on the basis of what's presented to them. (Clonmacken St., low take-up, community/comprehensive)

> What happens is that we have the home-school liaison officer in the school and he goes around the national schools in our catchment area and he outlines what subjects are available and our deputy principal [. . .] often goes around as well and sometimes teachers from those practical areas will go around as well. (Clonmacken St., low take-up, community/comprehensive)

> When they're coming into first year, we have an open day and next week we will have an open day here for the students that will be in fifth class in junior schools around the area. They'll be coming into the school here, they can see what's happening and they'll be able to see what's happening in every classroom. So they will have a good idea at that stage of what they may like. And also the students coming in will be addressed from the career guidance teacher in particular . . . [the guidance counsellor] goes around to the primary schools and gives a little talk on what the school provides and what subjects they'll be able to take and so on. (Southmead, high take-up, coed secondary)

Students' own perspectives on the adequacy of information provided on the different subject options will be discussed in Chapter Six.

4.3 FACTORS INFLUENCING STUDENTS' CHOICE OF JUNIOR CERTIFICATE SUBJECTS

Key personnel in the case-study schools were asked about the factors which they considered to influence students' choice of subjects at junior

cycle level. School staff mentioned a range of potential influences, including the attitude of the community students live in, their parents, siblings, peers, future career orientation, school and teachers.

Subject take-up was seen by some staff as reflecting the culture of
society in general and the school in particular, resulting in gendered patterns of subject take-up:

> Obviously you've got the whole historical perspective of what's
> been handed down in a particular school or area or whatever. I
> think it is reinforced in the media to a certain extent . . . that the
> woman is the home maker and the man goes out. It's changing
> but it's still there. But I think in terms of on the ground, in a
> school - I think the historical perspective has a huge role to play. I
> think it's very difficult to change the culture of any organisation,
> in particular a school, and I think single-sex schools introducing
> what's perceived as . . . a different type of subject into that can be
> quite difficult. (Park Lane, non-provision, girls' secondary)

Because of the marked gender differences in the take-up of technological
subjects in particular, this issue is discussed in greater detail in the following chapters of the study.

Parents

Key personnel saw parents as having a potentially strong influence on
students' subject choice. In some cases, it was felt that parents had already decided what subjects they would like their child to do before entry to the school, often on the basis of views about their child's future
career, and this was seen as prevailing over the student's own views:

> Sometimes they come in and their parents have decided what they
> want them to do. The decision is made at home before we talk to
> them really. I think here in our school because of the fact that we
> have a lot of follow through kids, that their brothers and sisters
> have been here earlier, the parents at that stage have decided the
> subjects they want their kids coming in to do and whether they
> want them to do Woodwork or not. And some coming in and they
> definitely want their kids to do Woodwork or Metalwork or

whatever and some I feel have made their decision not to. (Churchwood, high take-up, vocational)

The way it usually comes is . . . that the child likes a particular subject, the parents feel another subject would be more beneficial to them career-wise and often insist that the child do what they feel is best rather than what the child would like to do. And that's kind of sad from our point of view because we'd like to see the children do the things that they feel they're good at and they like to do. And I would say the subject that falls into that category most is Business, an awful lot of parents would wish their children to do Business Studies, maybe instead of Music, even though they might be very musical. Or instead of Art or instead of Woodwork, Metalwork, they want them to do Business. (Downend, low take-up, community/comprehensive)

Strongly held views about particular subjects on the part of parents was seen as reducing the potential for schools to encourage the choice of certain subjects among students. This pattern was seen as having particular implications for the potential for female students to select traditionally male technological subjects:

Take carpentry, for example. . . . You're a mother and you've a daughter and she wants to become an apprentice carpenter. You look up and you see "My God, do I want her roofing a house". . . . There's where the attitude has to be changed. [. . .] You know the attitude of parents, their knowledge of what the job opportunities are for girls if they go into a trade. (Oakleaf Ave., low take-up, vocational)

However, many of the key personnel felt that, while parents had some influence on subject choice, their influence was not necessarily dominant:

As a general rule parents wouldn't be hugely involved in seeking out information other than they would want to know the bottom line, if they don't do a particular subject at a particular level then they won't get into third level or whatever. (Park Lane, non-provision, girls' secondary)

> To my experience anyway generally they're [parents are] happy enough. Once the kids are happy enough, they're happy. (Churchwood, high take-up, vocational)

> Going on our last meeting with the parents of our incoming first years, a lot of parents . . . had a big say but I think the tail wags the dog in many houses in that our offspring do dictate at times, and they're usually influenced too by their peers. (Riversdale Lane, low take-up, vocational)

While parents are seen as a strong influence on subject choice, students were often see as being influenced by other students.

Peers

The peer group was considered another important factor influencing subject choice among junior cycle students and was more frequently mentioned by key personnel than other factors:

> Peer pressure, not so much peer pressure but peer choice, friends, who they think will be teaching them, that can very definitely be a consideration. (Southmead, high take-up, community/comprehensive)

Students who were unsure about their future direction or less self-confident, were seen as particularly influenced by their friends and peers:

> I think "word of mouth" might be something that certainly affects them, what has gone before, the feedback from there, I think maybe their friends' choices sometimes affects them but for the student who feels good about themselves and is fairly focused, that doesn't have the same impact on them. (Oldham Way, high take-up in TG and MT, coed secondary)

> You'll find that among students who are not aware of what they want to do really; the kind of student who won't devote time themselves individually to looking up, to going and seeing the guidance counsellor; the kind of student who wants things done for them; who is just not aware of what their own strengths and weaknesses are and what they want to do when they leave school.

You'll find that they will tend to go with where their friends are going, if they have a friend or a relative who is doing a course that sounds, I don't know, especially glamorous or earning lots of money and so on, they will tend to go with that as well. (Mountainview St., non-provision, girls' secondary)

It wouldn't be right across the board but for one or two students, yeah, they would have gone with their best pal. Their best pal might have decided well I want to do that, ah well I'll go along with you and that might happen. It's not right across the board because they're quite mature and again that will break down with the preferences they want. Then for a few who are not really sure what subjects they want to do, they'll take the choice on who is going into it, very, very few, in a class of twenty-four you might have two, it's not a huge thing but it does happen. (Churchwood, high take-up, vocational)

It was also felt that friendship groups played a stronger role in designated disadvantaged than in non-disadvantaged areas:

Parental influence in a disadvantaged area wouldn't be as great as in a middle-class area because most parents in a disadvantaged area don't have experience of post-primary education and what experience they would have would unfortunately tend to be negative. So it would be peers and that they do in and they like the teacher, they like her or like him yeah and we'll do that or they would hear from students in the other classes, we've Miss X for so and so and she's real cool, she's dead on, so they all want to do that. (Greenbank, non-provision, coed secondary)

"Word of mouth" about subjects from siblings or friends played a role in shaping student views about what subjects would be like and how easy they would be:

Sometimes what they hear from other students, their brothers or sisters or their friends who are in the school for a year or two. (Churchwood, high take-up, vocational)

Maybe their peers or their older brothers and sisters would be a big influence and maybe they'd be probably aware of how their results are going in these particular subject areas. . . . And peer pressure would be another thing, I'm sure that if there's a large number of girls or if there's a certain number, well then they're going to influence their friends when choices are being made at the beginning and I would say that that influences [them] a great deal. (Southmead, high take-up, community/comprehensive)

In one school with a taster programme, one staff member felt that friends became less influential when students had had a chance to try out a subject before making a final decision:

There is obviously an element of friends, what they're doing but we don't find that it's too big an influence. That basically when it does come down to the subjects that they enjoy or that they find when they've been doing the eight weeks that they are getting on well at. (Oldham Way, high take-up in TG and MT, coed secondary)

Future Career Orientation

A student's future career orientation was considered in general very important in determining their choice of subjects for the Junior Certificate:

Other influences will be if they have a notion of what career they want to go through to the future. (Southmead, high take-up, community/comprehensive)

One staff member saw technological subjects as particularly influenced by future career orientations as only students who considered a skilled manual occupation would select these subjects:

I would assume that most people who do let's say Woodwork, they do it with at the back of their mind that they're going to be carpenters or they're going to get benefit out of it. It's like they don't do Maths to be a mathematician or they don't do Science to be a scientist but yet if they do Woodwork they almost have this vision that if we do Woodwork we do it because we're going to work with wood later on. (Longwell Green, high take-up, vocational)

School and Teachers

Perhaps not surprisingly, key personnel in some schools identified the teacher as an important factor in students' decisions about which subjects to choose:

> What influences students to choose a subject is often the teacher. (Greenbank, non-provision, coed secondary)

This can represent a "positive" choice with students selecting subjects on the basis that they are taught by teachers that they like:

> And sometimes the teacher who is teaching a particular subject . . . they know what the teacher is like or whatever and they might opt "well I'd like to go there and do that", that kind of thing. (Churchwood, high take-up, vocational)

> Sometimes you see you might end up with a situation where a child is choosing their teacher rather than their subject and it may or may not be that that would be in fact the teacher for the subject the following year. (Downend, low take-up, community/comprehensive)

However, choices may also reflect students' desire to avoid being taught by a particular teacher:

> Now a lot of that [subject choice] would have to do with the sort of dynamics of the teacher. You see if the [subject] teacher isn't disposed to having the girls then the week you put him in with the girls, you know, . . . if you were doing a sort of classroom observe, you might well find that there would be sort of what I would consider politically incorrect implications in the message. And that certainly happens, I know that happens. (Glenveagh Road, low take-up, vocational)

In contrast to viewing teachers as a potential influence on subject choices among students, key personnel were much less likely to mention school structures or subject packaging as having an effect. One staff member did, however, relate choices to timetabling practices in the context of other influences such as teachers and perceived subject difficulty:

I'd say there's a number of influences, there would be the options and the way the options are stated to the kids, there would be the perceived background knowledge that students would have of teachers and how teachers would be perceived in the locality. There would be the perception of difficulties of the subject as well, so there would be three factors there that I would see. (Clonmacken St., low take-up, community/comprehensive)

The extent to which schools varied in the way they offered the technological subjects to students is considered in the following section.

4.5 CHOOSING TECHNOLOGICAL SUBJECTS

In addition to variation in the timing of subject choice, the case-study schools differed in how the technological subjects were allocated to (groups of) students and in how subject choices were packaged. Six of the case-study schools providing technological subjects divided students into base classes on the basis of their assessed ability. Previous research in the Irish context has indicated that the class to which students are allocated tends to have implications for the number and range of subjects they take (Smyth, 1999; Smyth et al., 2004). This pattern was also evident among the case-study schools with the subjects offered to students varying across classes in five of these schools. The main difference tended to centre on lower stream classes not having access to a foreign language. However, in four of the schools access to technological subjects is related to the class to which a student is assigned.

In three of these schools (Clonmacken St., Southmead and Churchwood), students in the lower stream classes are not offered Technical Graphics. This policy was based on the perceived difficulty of Technical Graphics for lower ability students:

Teacher: The students from the lower streams would generally not do Technical Graphics, the option is only offered to the first three streams of incoming first years for Graphics.

Interviewer: But do you think that the lower streams would be interested in doing the subjects?

Teacher: I think they would be interested but I think they would have great difficulty for Graphics.

Interviewer: Because of its nature?

Teacher: Because of its nature, it's a problem-solving subject. (Clonmacken St., low take-up of TG and MT, community/ comprehensive)

In both Longwell Green and Southmead, all students in lower stream classes were assigned Metalwork at junior cycle level. It could be argued that this practice may have a stigmatising effect in that the subject becomes seen as only suitable for lower ability students.

Allocation did not only play a role in subject take-up among lower stream classes. In both Churchwood and Longwell Green, every student was required to take Materials Technology (Wood); in Longwell Green, students were also required to take Home Economics, a policy that reflected school personnel's desire to provide students with appropriate life-skills:

> In this school Home Economics would be a set subject and our reasons for that is besides the education aspect and getting points in the Leaving Cert or whatever else, we're looking for the far greater educational needs and we would look at Home Economics for both boys and girls is equipping them for life and giving them a skill, a very important skill regardless of what results they get in their Junior Cert or Leaving Cert. (Longwell Green, high take-up, vocational)

Overall, three of the four case-study schools in which female take-up of technological subjects was relatively high allocated one technological subject to all or some students at junior cycle level. It should be noted, however, that for the optional technological subjects, timetabling meant that students in these schools were often required to choose between traditionally male and traditionally female subjects. Thus, gender stereotyping was clearly identifiable in the way subjects were timetabled. In

Churchwood school, Metalwork was timetabled against Home Economics and Technical Graphics against Art:[10]

> The way we have it timetabled here, it's Home Economics or Metalwork and its nearly perceived that the girls will do the Home Economics and the boys will do the Metalwork. (Churchwood, high take-up, vocational)

Similarly, in Longwell Green, Metalwork was timetabled against Business Studies and Technical Graphics against Art or French. In Southmead school, students in the lower stream classes were required to choose between Materials Technology and Home Economics. In the other "high take-up" school (Oldham Way), students follow a taster programme for eight weeks and are then required to pick two subjects from Materials Technology, Metalwork or Home Economics. This policy means that, even if they wish to, female students cannot "avoid" taking at least one traditionally male technological subject:

> We would have a choice of two out of three. Home Economics would be the other subject and virtually all of the girls would take Home Economics. There would be virtually no girl taking Technical Graphics and Woodwork as their two choices. So there still is perhaps an element of the traditional choices there. Because it's two out of three, so what would have been their uptake if they had a choice of not taking one of the technological subjects, I can't really say. But they [female students] don't seem to have any bother doing the Woodwork and are quite happy about doing it, and Technical Graphics, there's never been any complaint saying that I don't want to do either of those. They seem to be quite happy to take one [technological subject] up. (Oldham Way, high take-up of MT and TG, coed secondary)

The way in which the technological subjects are packaged varies among the schools in which female take-up of technological subjects is low. In Downend, students select four out of eight subjects before entering the school, try the four subjects for a year and then select two of the optional

---

[10] Art and Home Economics are generally perceived as "female subjects".

subjects for second year. In Clonmacken St., students (in the higher streams) select two subjects out of a list of six subjects before coming to the school. In both Glenveagh Road and Oakleaf Ave., subject packages tend to require students to select between traditionally male and traditionally female subjects. In Glenveagh Road, Metalwork is timetabled against Geography while Home Economics is timetabled against Materials Technology. In Oakleaf Ave., students are required to choose between taking all three technological subjects and taking Business Studies, Art and Home Economics. Such timetabling practices are seen as reflecting, as well as reinforcing, gender differences in the take-up of technological subjects:

> It's very difficult with the timetable . . . with small numbers you have to have clashes and you go with the majority. So Home Economics will be opposite Woodwork so you would end up not doing one or not doing the other. If the timetable wasn't an issue, I think . . . you certainly could get them [female students] into Technical Drawing . . . that wouldn't be a problem. (Oakleaf Ave., low take-up, vocational)

Although students are allowed to select subjects, their degree of choice may in fact be constrained by demand for particular subjects. The extent to which students' choices were constrained because certain subjects were oversubscribed will be discussed in Chapter Six when considering students' own views of the choice process.

4.6 CONCLUSIONS

Key personnel in the case-study schools saw the main influences on students' choice of subjects as being their family, friends, their future career orientation and their perceptions of subject teachers. The key role of parents in influencing young people's educational decisions is consistent with that found in other Irish research (Hannan et al., 1996; McCoy et al., forthcoming). The reliance on family and friends as sources of advice may reinforce gender stereotyping if parents are dependent on out-dated information about subjects in terms of the content of the syllabi and approaches used.

Differences across the school contexts were evident in the way in which the choice process was constructed. The case-study schools were found to vary in the timing of subject choice, the degree of choice afforded to students and timetabling practices regarding technological subjects. The schools differed in whether students were required to select their junior cycle subjects before entering the school or whether students were given the opportunity to try out subjects before selection. However, the timing of subject choice in itself did not differentiate between schools with a relatively high take-up of technological subjects among female students and those with a relatively low take-up. What appeared to distinguish between these two groups was the subject allocation and packaging policy of the school. In two of these schools, all students were required to study Materials Technology (Wood) while in one school, students in the lower streams were required to study Metalwork. In the remaining high take-up school, subject packaging was such that female students were required to select at least one traditionally male technological subject.

Where students were given a choice of subjects, subject packages were often gendered in nature with students required to directly choose between traditionally male and traditionally female subjects. This can be potentially be regarded as a cause and consequence of gender differences in subject take-up: timetable constraints mean that schools will package subjects on the basis of student demand (at least to some extent) but this process further facilitates gender stereotyping in subject take-up. The gendering of the technological subjects as "male" will be discussed in the following chapter while students' own perspectives on the factors influencing their choice of subjects will be presented in Chapter Six.

Chapter Five

GENDER DIFFERENCES IN THE TAKE-UP OF TECHNOLOGICAL SUBJECTS: THE PERSPECTIVE OF KEY PERSONNEL

5.1 INTRODUCTION

C hapter Four explored the ways in which the case-study schools structure the choice process and the potential influences on students' selection of subjects at junior cycle level. The most striking pattern in looking at the profile of students taking technological subjects is, however, the continuing persistence of marked gender differences in the take-up of Technical Graphics, Materials Technology (Wood) and Metalwork. This chapter draws on interviews with key personnel in the case-study schools to look at the potential reasons for the persistence of such gender differences. The second section looks at the potential obstacles to girls taking technological subjects. The third section explores the reasons why certain female students do choose "non-traditional" subjects while the fourth section examines possible ways of changing student and societal perceptions of technological subjects.

5.2 WHY DON'T GIRLS PURSUE TECHNOLOGICAL SUBJECTS?

Key personnel were asked about the potential barriers to girls taking the traditionally male technological subjects. One set of factors mentioned related to the gender stereotyping of certain subject areas or spheres of knowledge as "male" or "female" within society as a whole:

> I think it has been our culture. The trend has always been there.
> (Mountainview St., non-provision, girls' secondary)

This was seen as impacting on parental attitudes regarding the "appropri-ate" subjects to be taken by their child:

> It's not traditional for [the girls] really and I'd say from home influ-ence, they come in with pre-conceived ideas I think and some of them don't change. Traditionally it's probably more boys would have done it and it still hasn't changed around . . . there can be some of that still there. (Churchwood, high take-up, vocational)

> Well, you see my own personal opinion there has been so few role models at home in the home that it would never be mentioned; and funny enough, a lot of the kids and the families are very, for want of a word, Irish traditional: girls do this and boys do that. You'd imagine that would be gone in the modern day European country, it should be gone. (Clonmacken St., low take-up, community/comprehensive)

Parental conservatism about less traditional subject options for their chil-dren was seen as particularly evident where parents themselves did not have higher educational qualifications and/or were relying on a relatively out-of-date view of subject content:

> The problem is in many cases that we're not selling the subject to the students, we're selling it to the parents. Because, say, parents themselves who would have gone to secondary schools or commu-nity schools and who may not have done those subjects themselves, many of them wouldn't be *au fait* with what the subjects are like now. They still have the concept of what it was like maybe when they were in school twenty years ago. . . . What's on the syllabus now and how it's examined now; the fact that it's very much project based and design based and there's a lot of research and written re-port element to it. They still see the technological subjects as things where you go in and you saw wood and you make things . . . (Downend, low take-up, community/comprehensive)

A second set of factors related to the view that technological subjects were seen as attracting (only) those who wished to pursue a career in a skilled manual area. Given that these occupational groups are traditionally male, girls were seen as not choosing technological subjects because they did not intend to pursue these kinds of jobs in the future. Thus, gender differences in subject choice reflected existing patterns of occupational segregation by gender within the labour market:

> I think it's the whole traditional type mentality that it's a man's job to do carpentry, roofing, panel beating, become an engineer. It's still seen traditionally as a male job in lots of people's minds and even though there's been lots and lots of work to try and change people's perceptions in schools and outside of schools that the likes of engineering is not a male job, doesn't have to be, it still tends to be the preserve, I think, of mainly lads. Girls don't seem to want to go into it as much and again even though there has been a lot of emphasis on the fact that a girl can be a carpenter just as much as a lad can be. In my own career classes I would have shown videos, various videos on engineering and different types of engineering, one of them that just springs to mind is "Archimedes' Daughter" and it's promoting women in engineering, but still the whole mentality I think in general is that certain jobs are more male and other jobs are more female. (Churchwood, high take-up, vocational)

> [Girls] don't always pursue [a technological subject] because I'm sure the first thing they would want to know and that is the direction they're going. If they're not going into the trades that are going to use the subjects, they feel that they're not of huge benefit to them. (Longwell Green, high take-up, vocational)

In keeping with previous research (see, for example Riddell, 1992), younger students were seen as less likely to select non-traditional subject options than older students:

> I think at junior cycle girls probably because they don't see what future they have and they don't necessarily know what they're going to do in the Leaving Cert. I think once they do their Junior Cert, I think they have a much better idea of perhaps going into [the] engineering area. Quite a number of girls who wouldn't do technological subjects at Junior Cert would do them at Leaving Cert. (Glenveagh Road, low take-up in TG and MT, vocational)

A third set of factors related to the perceived nature and content of the technological subjects. Key personnel felt that students saw these subjects

as physically demanding with an unpleasant working environment in terms
of dirt and noise levels. In many ways, these perceptions reflected traditional stereotypes of some areas of manual work. Elements of the technological subjects were seen as requiring a certain amount of physical
strength:

> There are certain areas of technological subjects that, like in the
> construction area, say block work . . . which would be very physical.
> (Longwell Green, high take-up, vocational)

> Metalwork . . . it's seen, I wouldn't agree with it, but it's seen as a
> boys' subject, you need to be strong. (Glenveagh Road, low take-up
> in TG and MT, vocational)

In addition, students saw these subject areas as "dirty" and "noisy". Interestingly, Metalwork workshops in particular were characterised as being an
unpleasant environment for girls:

> When [girls] go into the Metalwork workshop . . . if the forge is go-
> ing and you've been cutting Perspex and it's fairly smelly in there as
> well. . . . OK, the timber smells okay but if you've first or second
> years after coming in after the sixth year students have been staining
> and stuff out in the storeroom and the smell would cut the nose off
> you as well, it doesn't always appeal to the girls, it is that little bit of
> it's a boys' subject. [So] the Metalwork is the biggest [gender] split
> here. (Churchwood, high take-up, vocational)

> We're fine in the first year when there's a little bit of timber [until],
> shall I say when it gets a little bit physically demanding and also
> we're fine until . . . when they need to have the nails right. . . .
> Sometimes they find that they don't like the broken fingernails, they
> don't like the bit of sawdust on the clothes. (Oakleaf Ave., low take-
> up, vocational)

However, some of the teachers highlighted the fact that the physical demands associated with the technological subjects and with traditionally
male occupations were a matter of perception rather than reality:

> There probably is a perception in Metalwork anyway that you get
> your hands dirty and maybe your nails broken or something and

again it's the wrong perception because it's not actually that physical. (Oakleaf Ave., low take-up, vocational)

How physically strong you are is not really going to make any difference if you want to be a civil engineer. You're not going to be really hauling heavy lumps of steel or concrete around the place if you're the engineer. OK, you'll be doing bits of it but . . . you're not going to be out there carrying a steel girder on your shoulder. So how physically strong you are is not going to be really important. So there's no reason why a girl can't become an engineer, why it's not more 50/50. I think it's just the whole mentality of the thing, that certain jobs are always seen as kind of male and other jobs are seen as female. (Churchwood, high take-up, vocational)

The perception that the technological subjects were physically demanding and dirty was seen by many teachers as accounting for girls' failure to take up these subjects. Allied to this was the fact that girls tended to underestimate their potential ability to do well in technological subjects:

It's just again to do with perception, they [girls] just don't see themselves being good in those areas and again I think it's a terrible pity. . . . I think they should all have some exposure to a technological subject. (Clonmacken St., low take-up, community/comprehensive)

Teacher attitudes were also seen as a potential barrier to subject take-up among female students:

I think that the only way that you can get them [girls] to take the technological subjects is to have a sympathetic teacher who is prepared to work with girls. Sometimes that can be a problem, practical people, particularly the older type that came from the trades background and maybe . . . coming directly from college nowadays, they don't see it as girls' place in the Woodwork room and I don't agree with that. (Glenveagh Road, low take-up in TG and MT, vocational)

The existing low take-up of technological subjects was seen as a barrier in itself with the consequent difficulty involved in girls being in a minority in a class:

I suppose it's intimidating for them really to go into [technological subjects], it's generally seen as a male environment, which it's not anymore and if a class of boys are doing it, it's very difficult for one girl to come into that class. (Glenveagh Road, low take-up in TG and MT, vocational)

Tradition is a factor, careers probably is a factor and I suppose another thing is if you're a girl in first year, you don't see girls in second year doing it and it kind of runs down the line. (Oakleaf Ave., low take-up, vocational)

While some teachers saw the potential obstacles as operating for all three technological subjects, many staff differentiated among the subjects in terms of their appeal to female students. One staff member felt that Technical Graphics was less stereotypically male in nature and overlapped to some extent with other subjects, such as Art, which had a traditionally high take-up among female students:

I think even from a name point of view — Technical Graphics — it doesn't have that same male bias as Metalwork and Woodwork . . . even just purely from that perspective. And I think the whole drawing element and I think there's not a lot between drawing and design, I think that it's probably an easier sell than Metalwork, Woodwork would be. (Park Lane, non-provision, girls' secondary)

More commonly, key personnel distinguished between Metalwork, which was seen as noisy and dirty, and Materials Technology (Wood), which was seen as "cleaner":

They're [girls] interested, I'd say they're more interested in Woodwork because it's maybe perceived to be a cleaner subject. Metalwork, you're doing welding and it's heavy lifting and big machinery. It can be noisy. (Churchwood, high take-up, vocational)

Woodwork tends to be more popular [with girls], Woodwork and Technical Graphics. Metalwork is inclined to be a bit more noisy when they're filling and hammering and drilling and that kind of thing and they would see it as being a little bit more, they're getting their hands more dirty if we like to put it that way, they tend to opt more for the Woodwork. (Churchwood, high take-up, vocational)

In sum, parental attitudes to technological subjects, the association between technological subjects and traditionally male occupational areas along with the labelling of technological subjects as physically demanding, dirty and noisy were seen by key personnel as potential barriers to girls choosing technological subjects. The following section considers the perceived characteristics of girls who do opt to take these subjects.

5.3 WHY DO GIRLS CHOOSE TECHNOLOGICAL SUBJECTS?

Key personnel identified a number of factors which increased the likelihood of students, both male and female, taking technological subjects at junior cycle level. Firstly, having a direct family connection with skilled manual work was seen as orienting students towards technological subjects at school and training routes such as apprenticeship on leaving school. Students were seen as more likely to take these subjects if they already aspired to craft-related work in the future:

> I think a lot of it depends on the students' background, the home environment they came from. A lot of boys and girls . . . want to carry on trade subjects and this would be a natural instinct they would have acquired from either uncles, aunts or fathers or home environment. (Longwell Green, high take-up, vocational)

> You've some very bright sparks take up the technological subjects because (a) they've a yen for it or (b) there's a tradition in a family or (c) they see themselves down the road doing something career wise that involves Engineering, Metalwork, Building Construction, Woodwork, I'm joining subjects together now, or Technical Graphics, Technical Drawing, in the sense of architecture, apprenticeships and so on. They have a rationale behind it. . . . Boys of thirteen, fourteen, see themselves being mechanics so they'll take up Metalwork because that's what they like, they like doing things with their hands and they're good with their hands. It's most to do with background there. (Riversdale Lane, low take-up, vocational)

A second reason for choosing technological subjects was the hands-on nature of the subjects as an alternative to more traditional academic subjects, allowing for more activity, interaction and freedom within the classroom context:

> I think it's [Metalwork] one of these subjects that [the students] not stuck sitting in a seat all the time, they can get up and they can move around and they can talk and they're not tied down. They've rules but the rules aren't basically you have to be quiet, you have to take down all the notes. There is a little bit more freedom for them to have a little bit more input in what they're doing . . . it's not all just teacher orientated. (Riversdale Lane, low take-up, vocational)

> [The students] enjoy the thrill, maybe they do a little bit of carpentry at home or their dad or maybe their friends or their uncles or their parents "tinker" around with the inside of cars or whatever, so there is a perception that among some that a technological subject will be a more enjoyable subject because it's more hands on. (Southmead, high take-up, community/comprehensive)

> I think [there are] certainly areas that [the students] like and they enjoy and the fact that they are subjects that have a different focus in class compared to say languages or Maths or Science, then that's one of the appealing factors. There's a bit of movement in class, different approach to work on that subject as well and that's a nice option to vary the day. (Oldham Way, high take-up in TG and MT, coed secondary)

Similar reasons were advanced for explaining why girls would choose these traditionally male subjects. Firstly, some key personnel saw family tradition as playing an important role in motivating girls to take technological subjects. Interestingly, all of the teachers concerned mentioned fathers rather than mothers as role models, reflecting the persistence of gender segregation in craft occupations and hence the lack of potential female role models for girls.

> I'm not sure, maybe some of them . . . their dads might be handy at home and maybe relatives have businesses in those areas or maybe they were getting extensions or buildings at home and they liked what they saw the men working at. (Downend, low take-up, community/comprehensive)

I know a particular girl that because her dad is a bricklayer and stonemason, she has followed in his footsteps and she's wonderful at it. . . . It does happen, I think first year students are moulded a lot by what the parents have done and their way in life and it's really their first learning and that sets them up. (Longwell Green, high take-up, vocational)

Some girls . . . just particularly want to do it, they have seen their father maybe involved in something and some of them maybe helped their fathers at home when they're younger and they're mad to come up here and do Woodwork and some do terribly well. (Churchwood, high take-up, vocational)

Secondly, future career orientation was also seen as predictive of taking up technological subjects among female students:

You have quite a few girls gone into the trades area and they pursue electrical, now I've had girls that I presented for a competition, young engineer competition at Leaving Cert. (Longwell Green, high take-up, vocational)

Family networks and aspirations appear to be inter-connected, whereby students are more likely to consider technological areas if there is a role model in their immediate family or community.

The novelty of the subject and its hands-on nature were also mentioned as motivating factors by some key personnel:

I think also some of the girls will choose, it's different I suppose and a temptation to any kids coming in, it's a new subject, it's Woodwork we can do, we've never done it before, I think a lot of them will definitely come in and will do a new subject because it's a new subject, even if they don't know anything about it at all. (Churchwood, high take-up, vocational)

However, two staff members felt that some female students selected technological subjects merely to be in a class with a predominance of boys:

Some girls take it up because they need it very badly and are into technological subjects and into Art and a few girls just take it up because they want to be with boys, which is the wrong reason. (Riversdale Lane, low take-up, vocational)

Unfortunately some of them [girls] come for the wrong reasons I'm afraid but some of them come and are very good and really do enjoy it. Sometimes you get a very weak girl that comes and they will almost come to the school to do Woodwork and Metalwork if possible because they're in boys' classes at that time and they are not going to make much progress anyway, they will come for the totally wrong reasons. Some of them but now I couldn't say that's a very general thing. (Churchwood, high take-up, vocational)

Some staff members felt that there had been changes over time in the take-up of technological subjects on the part of female students:

A lot would have changed, a lot more would want to do it now, a lot of girls, even the good girls, very bright girls before may not have done Woodwork and now they will so it's changed that way, I think. (Churchwood, high take-up, vocational)

Well they're very much definitely male dominated but not at all to the same extent as they used to be in the past, I've seen huge strides over the years in terms of students choosing. . . . So it is a situation that's changing rapidly over the last number of years and there are no longer taboos and similarly there are a significant number of boys who choose Home Economics. I'm in this game a long time, I've been doing this a long time and certainly back 10 or 15 years ago it would be unusual to find a boy in a Home Economic class, it would be very unusual to find a girl in a Woodwork class or a Metalwork class or a Technical Graphics class. But there's been a huge change, but they're still somewhat male dominated but not at all to the same extent. (Longwell Green, high take-up, vocational)

I think that women have become more liberated and I think they're far more advanced in their thinking as well and they have greater encouragement from home and they have got young parents now who are encouraging them, saying "why don't you do Science?" and I think this old factor of years ago "no don't, do Home Economics", I think it's going. (Mountainview St., non-provision, girls' secondary)

The extent to which gender differences in the take-up of technological sub-jects are amenable to change is taken up in the following section.

5.4 CAN GENDER STEREOTYPING BE CHALLENGED?

Having female role models in traditionally male subjects and occupational areas was seen as a possible way of breaking down barriers. In a number of cases, the school staff stressed the importance of positive role models and greater availability of information in informing students' opinions of certain subjects:

> I think you need role models, they have a big role to play, you need somebody that they can aspire to being, I think that works because it's lonely being the first one to change or whatever. You need some kind of leader who is going to bring four or five students with them and decide this is what we want to do and that they have a role model in mind and a follow on after it. . . . A well known person in a particular area would certainly, even if the celebrity if you want to call it that, is no longer using what they actually studied, so if you had whatever television personality who did Technical Graphics and went on to do something else in the art world or whatever, that you could sell it easier I think as a kind of a starting off point. (Park Lane, non-provision, girls' secondary)

> I think part of the problem is a lack of awareness in that for example they haven't been exposed to the possibilities of what Woodwork is, what Metalwork is, what the career opportunities are, how many female students are already working in the area. That's what needs to be done. (Mountainview St., non-provision, girls' secondary)

> Although we do a lot of work on explaining to them the value of like Technical Drawing in careers that they could be interested in, I still think that that is an area that is not clear enough. . . . I think that that does need to be presented in a much clearer way, that there are people who would be doing, females who would be doing these jobs. I think there is a lack of role models there. (Oldham Way, high take-up in TG and WW, coed secondary)

Having female teachers of technological subjects was also seen as potentially having a positive effect on take-up:

> From next year on we will have a Metalwork teacher who is a fe-
> male. . . . So she'll be teaching Metalwork, Engineering, Woodwork
> or whatever else, so she'll be very good as regards a role model in
> that area for girls. (Longwell Green, high take-up, vocational)

Changing patterns of subject take-up were seen as following on from
changes in broader work patterns in the wider society:

> The tradition of [perceiving subjects in a certain way] then will
> change, that instead of you being in a household where your father
> is the engineer and your mother is the nurse, if it was the other way
> around, well then the girl in that family is more likely to say well
> my mother is an engineer, I can become an engineer or I can be-
> come a nurse either, father is a nurse. Yeah, I think it's only when
> that changes like that, when you do have different role models in the
> house or in your street or wherever . . . it's when that starts to
> change that more girls will go in. I think we could put on videos all
> day every day about the opportunities for girls in engineering or in
> construction, maybe kind of more towards carpentry and all that but
> I don't think it's going to make any difference until they see it hap-
> pening outside on the street with people that they know. . . . It will
> take a long, long time I think for the perception of that to change.
> (Churchwood, high take-up, vocational)

A more proactive policy on the part of schools was also seen as potentially
reducing subject stereotyping. Schools could raise awareness of technological subjects by providing information for students and their parents during
induction programmes and information days/nights organised for new students in post-primary schools:

> We deal with [subject choice] on the information night, always
> comes up. Parents will ask can boys do this, can girls do that, be-
> cause many of our parents would have themselves come through
> pretty stereotype single sexed education themselves and that would
> be well founded perceptions that they would have. Sometimes
> they're asking, I've a boy, is he allowed to do Home Economics or

I've a girl, is it possible that she could do Woodwork or whatever. So we would advise not only are they allowed but we would encourage them to do so and I suppose we would certainly outline on the information evening outcomes in terms of careers. I can't see any reason in the world why you can't have a female architect as well as a male architect or draughtsperson or, lots of the television programmes you'll see, the cookery programmes on television and so on, generally tend to be men presenting them with the few exceptions here and there. (Downend, low take-up, community/comprehensive)

One staff member felt that having a taster programme helped to some extent to break down a stereotyped view of the subject:

And there is still a bias, like I said we get the odd one or two who will come in and say "this is a boys' subject", it's not perceived as being for girls. Now it's fine once they get something to bring home to mammy, they're as happy as Larry, that they've made something, that they can see the value for it then but when they come in initially they do tend to think of it as a boys' subject. (Churchwood, high take-up, vocational)

However, many key personnel saw the change process as extremely slow and stereotyping as highly resistant to intervention on the part of schools:

Definitely I would say that they need role models . . . and about twelve years ago we had a girl here doing Leaving Cert and she was brilliant, absolutely brilliant, in Engineering and Technical Drawing. And we thought at that time that she was a role model, that things were going to open up, it didn't but having said that we do need role models yes, it's a culture that needs to be changed. (Oakleaf Ave., low take-up, vocational)

We would do our best to break down those stereotypical perceptions and open possibilities for students and I think it's working to some degree but it's a slow process. It's quite slow, there are boys doing Home Economics and there are girls doing the Woodwork, Metalwork and Drawing but in very limited numbers, there wouldn't nearly be half and half or anything like that. Girls would still quite definitely be, both the majority taking Home Economics and the minority taking the other subjects. (Downend, low take-up, community/comprehensive)

In sum, key personnel saw the availability of female role models in non-traditional areas along with increased promotion of technological subjects as having the potential to reduce gender differences in subject take-up. However, many were cautious about the potential for schools to change these patterns in isolation from broader societal change.

5.5 CONCLUSIONS

Key personnel identified a number of potential barriers to girls' participation in technological subjects including societal attitudes, parental perceptions of gender-appropriate subjects and the delineation of technological subjects as physically demanding, noisy and dirty. Stereotypical views of the subjects were seen as impacting on the take-up of Metalwork in particular. In addition, technological subjects were seen as leading naturally on to apprenticeships and craft-related jobs. While this was an attraction for some female students, existing occupational stereotyping within skilled manual work was seen as having a negative effect on girls' willingness to take up technological subjects.

Having a family tradition in craft-related jobs along with the activity-based nature of classes were seen as attracting students, both male and female, to the technological subjects. Some key personnel felt there had been a decline in subject stereotyping over time and that further change could follow on from having more female role models in non-traditional areas and schools taking a more proactive role in promoting technological subjects. However, staff were cautious about the extent to which intervention at the school level alone could be successful.

Chapter Six

STUDENTS' PERSPECTIVES ON SUBJECT CHOICE

6.1 INTRODUCTION

Interviews were conducted with groups of students in order to explore issues relating to subject choice in their schools. Girls and boys were interviewed separately. In schools providing technological subjects, a group of female students who were taking Metalwork, Materials Technology (Wood) and/or Technical Graphics, a group of female students who were not taking any of the three technological subjects and a group of male students were interviewed. Students in the case-study schools were asked to reflect on their experiences regarding subject choice at junior cycle level. This chapter explores the main themes that emerged from the interviews. Section two looks at students' perceptions of the choice process, discussing their access to information regarding the different subjects. Section three explores students' satisfaction with how choice was structured, in particular examining whether their choice of subjects was constrained. The fourth section looks at the influences on subject choice among students while the fifth section focuses more specifically on factors shaping gender differences in the take-up of technological subjects.

6.2 STUDENT PERCEPTIONS OF THE CHOICE PROCESS: THE NATURE AND TIMING OF CHOICE

Chapter Four highlighted variation across the case-study schools in the timing of subject choice and consequently in the kind of information provided to students on the different subject options. Students in schools where they chose their subjects before or on entry tended to report receiving little information and advice on the available subject options:

> Interviewer: So was there any advice from the school as to what subjects would be like?
>
> Girl: No, not really. (Girls taking technological subjects, Churchwood, high take-up, vocational)

In most cases, students in these schools received information during the school open day (or evening) when students and their parents could familiarise themselves with the school. In some cases, this was accompanied by written information on subject choices sent to the students' homes:

> Boy: Open day, that's about it.
>
> Boy: Open day, you could look around the classroom.
>
> Interviewer: But none of the teachers spoke to you and said this is what the subject is going to be like?
>
> Boy: No, we got a letter at home saying . . . what subjects . . . [we could choose from]. (Male students, Riversdale Lane, low take-up, vocational)

Some of these students reported that they would have liked to receive more information about the available subject choices before making their decision:

> Interviewer: Do you think that you would have liked to get more information about the subjects?
>
> Boy: Be easier to choose then. (Male students, Riversdale Lane, low take-up, vocational)
>
> Boy: You would have known what you were doing, what it was about. (Male students, Southmead, high take-up, community/ comprehensive)

Students in schools with a taster programme had some exposure to the content of the various subjects before making a decision and were also more likely to report receiving information and advice from school staff:

> Boy: The teachers said what they [subjects] would be like if we did them. (Male students, Oldham Way, high take-up in TG and MT, coed secondary)

> Interviewer: Were you given any advice as to which subjects to choose?

> Girl: Take Science because you can't get into college without Science. [The guidance counsellor] was in charge of it but then we kind of asked the rest of our teachers. (Female students, Park Lane, non-provision, girls' secondary)

However, even in these schools, access to formal guidance was seen as somewhat limited:

> Girl: We never really went [to the guidance counsellor], it was for the older years, about career and all that.

> Girl: It didn't matter to me but maybe to other students it did. (Female students taking Technical Graphics, Oldham Way, high take-up in TG and MT, coed secondary)

> Girl: Not necessarily, it was just left to your own choice really.

> Girl: We'd done a lot in class.

> Girl: Yeah it was something like a kind of a course thing between the three classes and then at the end of the term we got to pick which classes we wanted between Woodwork, Home Ec and Technical Graphics.

> Interviewer: Did you talk about the choice with somebody in your family or in the school?

> Girl: . . . I think we all did just what we'd rather do, instead of sitting somewhere where you didn't want to do [the subject]. (Female students taking Materials Technology (Wood), Oldham Way, high take-up in TG and MT, coed secondary)

It should be noted that in both schools with early subject choice and those with taster programmes, students primarily reported relying on informal sources of advice, such as parents, siblings and friends, in making decisions about subject choice (see section 5.4).

Where students expressed a preference regarding the timing of subject choice, many considered the taster programme as potentially useful in helping them decide which subjects to select. This view was apparent among those in schools which did not provide a sampling approach as well as in schools where a taster programme was already in place:

> Boy: You get to try out the subjects for a period of weeks, when you first come into the school you try out the subjects and then whatever you like you pick and whatever you don't like you leave. (Male students, Oldham Way, high take-up in TG and MT, coed secondary)

> Girl: Yeah, [students in another school in the area] try out things, they do everything in the year, in first year they do all subjects, I think it's better to do that because then you can pick what you like and see what you're better at.

> Girl: So that way you can see what they're like and get to pick what you really want to do. (Female students taking Materials Technology, Riversdale Lane, low take-up, vocational)

> Girl: I think it's [taster approach] better . . . [another local school] do it and in first year they do all the subjects to see what subjects they want to do for their Junior Cert. (Female students taking technological subjects, Southmead, high take-up, community/comprehensive)

This situation was contrasted against the lack of information available for students who had to decide on (some of) their subjects before entry to the school:

> I didn't like it because you didn't know what the classes were like before you had picked them, you didn't know what teachers . . . (Female students not taking technological subjects, Downend, low take-up, community/comprehensive)

Overall, students in the case-study schools reported relatively limited access to formal information on subject content before making their choices for the junior cycle. In keeping with previous research (Smyth et al., 2004), students tended to express a preference for having the chance to try out different subjects before making their final selection.

6.3 STUDENT PERCEPTIONS OF THE CHOICE PROCESS: HOW MUCH CHOICE IS ALLOWED?

Non-provision of technological subjects

Three of the case-study schools, two girls' secondary schools and one coeducational secondary school, did not provide Technical Graphics, Materials Technology (Wood) or Metalwork. Students in these schools were asked if they would take these subjects if they were available.

Boys in Greenbank were keen on the idea of taking technological subjects, especially Materials Technology (Wood), because they were seen as "boys' subjects":

> It would be better for us [to have technological subjects] because we're better at them, we're better at that kind of stuff. (Male students, Greenbank, non-provision, coed secondary)

Some female students expressed similarly gender-stereotyped views of the technological subjects and Home Economics:

> Girl: When you say Home Ec you straightaway think girls' subject, you don't think boys' subject.

> Girl: And then when you think Woodwork, it's automatically boys. (Female students, Mountainview St., non-provision, girls' secondary)

In particular, some female students voiced their reluctance to take technological subjects because they lead on to the kind of jobs they would not be interested in:

> Girl: I wouldn't take any of them [technological subjects] . . . be-
> cause we wouldn't be a carpenter or anything.

> Girl: It's just a waste of time then if you think about it in one
> way, because you're not going to go out making [cabinets] . . .
> and stuff like that. (Female students, Park Lane, non-provision,
> girls' secondary)

Perceived difficulty of these subjects also played a role in students' reluctance to take up (some of the) technological subjects:

> Interviewer: Would you choose any of those three [technological
> subjects]?

> Girl: Probably the Technical Graphics.

> Interviewer: And why would you prefer that to the others?

> Girl: I wouldn't like Woodwork and Metalwork.

> Interviewer: Why is that?

> Girl: It's too hard. (Female students, Park Lane, non-provision,
> girls' secondary)

Some of the students reported a lack of familiarity with the content of the
technological subjects and a number felt they might be interested in taking technological subjects, provided they had a chance to try them out
before making their decision:

> Girl: [I would like to] try them first.

> . . .

> Girl: [I would like to] try them and see if I like them. (Female
> students, Park Lane, non-provision, girls' secondary)

> Girl: I'd like to try it [Metalwork] out to see what it was like in-
> stead of doing a subject that I dislike. (Female students, Moun-
> tainview St., non-provision, girls' secondary)

However, some female students challenged the stereotyped views expressed by other students and felt they would take up technological subjects if given the opportunity:

Girl: And Home Economics is more so for girls, it seems like

Girl: Because you've the cooking and cleaning stuff.

Girl: But lads can still cook, just because they're boys it doesn't mean they can't cook and girls can still do Woodwork as well . . .

Girl: So I think they should be introduced to the school.

Girl: Definitely. (Female students, Mountainview St., non-provision, girls' secondary)

Girl: I'd like to do Metalwork.

. . .

Girl: All the boys' schools and the mixed schools do that because more boys would choose Woodwork or Tech Graph or anything like that. If I was in a mixed school I probably would have chosen one of them.

Interviewer: So what do you think Metalwork would be like?

Girl: I don't know, I just think it would be interesting making stuff.

Girl: It's like a lad's version of Home Ec.

Girl: Well I think that would be pretty cool and I'd prefer the school to have it at least because it's not like this isn't a boys' school so we can't have all boy things but they're not really, girls could do it too. (Female students, Mountainview St., non-provision, girls' secondary)

In sum, in the three case-study schools not providing the technological subjects, male students indicated an unambiguous desire to have such subjects introduced into their school. In contrast, views were more mixed among female students with some expressing a reluctance to take these subjects while others were more positive about the prospect.

Constrained choice?

Chapter Four outlined differences among the case-study schools in how open choices were for (groups of) first year students. In some schools, the degree of choice related to the class to which students were allocated while in other schools the actual choices open to students were relatively limited. A number of students in the case-study schools expressed dissatisfaction with the combination or types of subjects they could choose from. In some instances, this related to the packaging of subjects while the lack of provision of certain subjects was also raised as an issue:

> Boy: You only got to choose two [subjects] and that was it, the rest you were made do. There was a choice between Metalwork and Business Studies.

> Boy: Metalwork and Business Studies, Art, French or TG. If you wanted to do Art and French, you couldn't do it. You can just do one of them.

> Boy: There was no History or Geography. Yeah, I would have done History as well. (Male students, Longwell Green, high take-up, vocational)

In Churchwood and Oldham Way, a number of students felt that the degree of choice allowed was rather limited:

> Boy: You were given lists of subjects we had to do, you had to do History and Woodwork.

> Boy: We were given our timetable. And we only had a choice between Metalwork and Home Ec and TG and Art. (Male students, Churchwood, high take-up, vocational)

> Girl: We got eight weeks to try out the three subjects.

> Girl: Well we didn't really get a big choice, there was only three subjects and you had to pick two of them so one is gone. (Female students taking Technical Graphics, Oldham Way, high take-up in TG and MT, coed secondary)

In schools where students had a choice of subjects, students did not necessarily receive their first choice as some subjects were over-subscribed. This was reported by some students in five of the case-study schools (Downend, Clonmacken St., Southmead, Mountainview St. and Glenveagh Road):

> Girl: I wanted to do Home Ec but . . . no room left. (Female students taking Materials Technology and/or Metalwork, Southmead, high take-up, community/comprehensive)

> Girl: You have a list and you just write your favourite two [subjects], in order like first, second, third, fourth. And then the ones that you most like sometimes you get them and sometimes you don't. (Female students not taking technological subjects, Clonmacken St., low take-up, community/comprehensive)

> Girl: I've older brothers and they all told me to pick Woodwork. I picked Woodwork but I didn't get into the class, there was too many in the class. (Female students taking technological subjects, Southmead, high take-up, community/comprehensive)

This sometimes meant that students were unhappy with the subjects they had to take for the Junior Certificate and "got put into stuff that they didn't really want to do". (Female students taking technological subjects, Southmead, high take-up, community/comprehensive)

In one school, Glenveagh Road, students reported that the school reacted to certain subjects being over-subscribed by assigning students to subject options on the basis of their gender:

> Girl: [The choice was between] Woodwork and Home Ec and Metalwork and Geography.

> Girl: About sixty students wanted to do Metalwork and only five people wanted to do Geography.

> Girl: So they had to split it, so the girls did Geography, the boys Metalwork

> Girl: And only two boys are doing Geography and none of the girls are doing Metalwork. (Female students not taking technological subjects, Glenveagh Road, low take-up, community/comprehensive)

Students reported that the only exception to this allocation pattern came about because of parental intervention:

Girl: [A fellow student — she was allowed to] go to Metalwork and it was a whole boys' class and she was the one person that was allowed go there. I think her dad came to the school or something. And she ended up going to Geography then after a while because she was the only girl there. (Female students not taking technological subjects, Glenveagh Road, low take-up, community/comprehensive)

This situation was seen as highly unfair by some of the female students, although one asserted that male students were more likely to "use" Metalwork in the future:

Interviewer: And why do you think they [allocated the subjects] that way?

Girl: They [the staff] think that the boys are better.

Girl: They'd [boys] use it [Metalwork] more than girls probably.

Interviewer: Do you think there would have been a fairer way to do it?

Girl: Yeah. Take half the girls and half the boys. (Female students not taking technological subjects, Glenveagh Road, low take-up, community/comprehensive)

In sum, there was variation across the case-study schools in the subject choices open to students. In addition, because of differential demand for subjects, certain subject areas were over-subscribed and students in some schools were not allocated to the classes they had selected.

6.4 INFLUENCES ON SUBJECT CHOICE

Students in the case-study schools were asked to reflect on the factors that most influenced their choice of subjects for the Junior Certificate and about the sources of advice they had drawn on in making their decision. Students often mentioned a combination of influences, although they tended to rely more on informal sources of advice (parents, siblings and friends) rather than formal sources (such as teachers and guidance counsellors).

Parents were seen by many students, both male and female, as an important influence in decisions made about subject take-up at junior cycle level, a finding that is consistent with other national research (Hannan et al., 1996; McCoy et al., forthcoming). However, students varied in the extent to which they felt that they themselves or their parents had made the ultimate decision. In some cases, parents were seen as determining the selection of subjects on the part of students:

Interviewer: Were there other subjects also that you would have considered taking?

Girl: Yeah, I wanted to do Metalwork.

Interviewer: Why are you then not doing Metalwork?

Girl: Because my mother wouldn't let me.

Interviewer: What did she say?

Girl: She wanted me to do Science instead. (Female students taking technological subjects, Riversdale Lane, low take-up, vocational)

Boy: My parents picked my subjects for me, [I] didn't get to choose. (Male students, Riversdale Lane, low take-up, vocational)

Girl: My Da told me that Home Ec was for dossers and I wasn't to do it.

Interviewer: Oh right, do you regret that you didn't take it?

Girl: Yeah.

Interviewer: What did you take instead?

Girl: Metalwork. (Female students taking technological subjects, Churchwood, high take-up, vocational)

Underlying concern about students' future career options appeared to play a role in parents' wanting their children to pursue certain subject options. In particular, Business Studies was mentioned as a subject that was viewed favourably by parents:

Girl: Yeah, my Mam and dad really wanted me to do a business subject. They were saying there's not much you can do without business. I wanted to do dancing as a career and there's no subjects in school I can choose for dancing and they're saying oh well if you don't do dancing you need something to fall back on. I don't really want to do anything really with business because I just don't like it and it gets complicated, when we're doing if you own a shop and there's so much you have to do.

Interviewer: What about you?

Girl: Yeah my Mam and dad wanted me to pick business, so I picked business and Art because if I did one serious subject then Art could be like a fun subject. (Female students, Mountainview St., non-provision, girls' secondary)

Girl: I really liked Woodwork but my parents wanted me to do Business Studies. Yeah, they said it would probably be more useful. (Female students not taking technological subjects, Downend, low take-up, community/comprehensive)

Sometimes parents advised their children to pick a subject of practical value or the one they had resources for:

Girl: My Ma told me to pick Spanish because we go away to Spain every year. (Female students, Greenbank, non-provision, coed secondary)

Boy: Well I was going to do Metalwork in first year but my dad said we've got all the equipment at home to do Woodwork and stuff, we don't have any metal machines or any metal so it would be better to do Woodwork. (Male students, Downend, low take-up, community/comprehensive)

While some parents had definite views about subjects their children should be doing, others expressed a more *laissez-faire* attitude:

Girl: My Ma and Da didn't care [what subjects I picked]. (Female students taking technological subjects, Southmead, high take-up, community/comprehensive)

Girl: I was talking to my Mam and dad and they just said take whatever you want to take, because you're going to be doing it for the first three years, so take what you think you'll be able to do. (Female students taking Technical Graphics, Oldham Way, high take-up in TG and WW, coed secondary)

Interviewer: Did you discuss it [subject choice] with anybody at home what to do?

Boy: Yeah, my Ma asked me what I picked and I just told her. (Male students, Greenbank, non-provision, coed secondary)

In other cases, parents had less influence on subject choice and students' preferences overrode those of their parents:

Girl: My Mam and dad wanted me to pick business but I just said I don't want to do it, I know I'm not going to have a career with business, so they just said yeah that's fine. (Female students, Mountainview St., non-provision, girls' secondary)

Girl: Yeah my Da was trying to make me do stuff I didn't want to.

Interviewer: What would you have liked to do?

Girl: The stuff I'm doing now, I changed them [the choices]. (Female students, Southmead, high take-up, community/ comprehensive)

Interviewer: So what kind of subjects did your parents want you to do?

Girl: Business, I don't know why. I just pretended I picked it and I just said I didn't get it. [general laughter]

Girl: I was so tempted to do that. (Female students, Mountain-view St., non-provision, girls' secondary)

In addition to the influence from parents, students' decisions regarding subject choice were also informed by their older siblings and friends:

Girl: I asked my brother and he said that Woodwork was good. (Female students taking technological subjects, Riversdale Lane, low take-up, vocational)

Boy: My brother told me . . .

Boy: I asked my sister and my brother. They just gave me the good [subjects] and the bad ones.

Interviewer: How did you know what subject to tick off?

Boy: Because I asked my friend next door. (Male students, Southmead, high take-up, community/comprehensive)

Older students in the school were also seen as a valuable source of information regarding the subjects on offer and the teachers students would be likely to have:

Interviewer: Did you get any advice as to what subjects to pick?

Girl: You could ask the older years, when you were in first year and you could just ask what do you think is the best subject, how do you get along and all that but it's really your own choice whether you want to do it or not. (Female students taking Technical Graphics, Oldham Way, high take-up in TG and MT, coed secondary)

Interviewer: Who gave you advice?

Girl: People just said don't pick Science because the teacher is a moan and all. (Female students, Greenbank, non-provision, coed secondary)

A number of students selected subjects because of an underlying interest in the subject or a feeling that they would be good at a particular subject:

Interviewer: What influenced your choice most of all?

Girl: What we were capable of doing.

Interviewer: So you kind of picked the subjects that you were good at?

Girl: Yeah. . . . Thought we were going to be good at. (Female students taking technological subjects, Oldham Way, high take-up in TG and MT, coed secondary)

Interviewer: How did you know what to pick?

Girl: They were my two favourite subjects. (Female students taking Materials Technology, Downend, low take-up, community/comprehensive)

Boy: I liked the subjects so I picked them. People would tell me that they're good subjects.

Boy: I just wanted to see whether I'd like them. (Male students, Southmead, high take-up, community/comprehensive)

One female student chose Materials Technology because of the interest she had developed from working with her father:

Girl: My dad is a carpenter and everything and I just enjoyed it when we used to do it at home in the shed in the back garden and I did it when I came into the school just to try it out and I really enjoyed it. I just like the whole idea of crafting something and then being able to take it home. (Female students taking Materials Technology, Downend, low take-up, community/comprehensive)

Others saw the technological subjects as drawing on their artistic and creative skills and interests:

Interviewer: Why Technical Graphics?

Girl: Because it was similar to Art and I liked it.

Interviewer: Why Woodwork?

Girl: Because I like being creative. (Female students taking Materials Technology, Downend, low take-up, community/comprehensive)

Both male and female students mentioned choosing technological subjects because they were more active subjects and different in nature to traditional academic subjects:

Interviewer: Why would you like technological subjects?

Boy: Easier to do.

Boy: Less boring.

Boy: You use your hands.

Boy: It's using your hands, it's better than sitting in a classroom all day.

Boy: When you're in your Woodwork class or Metalwork class you can walk around.

Boy: You can enjoy yourself.

Boy: In a normal class you can't.

Boy: You just sit there.

Boy: You can't speak either in a normal class. (Male students, Riversdale Lane, low take-up, vocational)

Girl: There aren't as many "sit there and be quiet" kind of rules in Woodwork as there would in English, Geography, History, all them, you'd do your work but you could do it while chatting to your friends. (Female students taking Materials Technology, Downend, low take-up, community/comprehensive)

Girl: I kind of find it relieving that we can go to Art or go to Woodwork or whatever subject and feel at ease. You're not all up tight as oh here's another subject I have to have homework for. You can kind of be yourself more in it and be more artistic or whatever in whatever way. (Female students taking technological subjects, Downend, low take-up, community/comprehensive)

In a number of cases, future career orientation influenced students' choice of subjects, although their career preferences sometimes changed subsequently:

Girl: Yeah, I knew that I didn't want to be a business woman, I knew that I didn't want to do business, I thought it would be cool to be an artist so I picked Art and I thought I'd really like to be a chef so I picked Home Ec, I don't really want to be a chef or an artist now but.

Girl: . . . and now I really don't like it [Business Studies] and I don't want to be a business woman. I just picked Business because I thought I'd like it. But I don't. (Female students, Mountainview St., non-provision, girls' secondary)

In schools where taster programmes allowed students to try out a number of different subjects, it was possible to drop some subjects at the end of the "taster" period. The reasons for dropping certain subjects varied, including perceptions of the teacher, views on the content of the subjects and parental perceptions:

Girl: I dropped Art and Technical Graphics for the teacher was terrible.

Girl: I dropped Technical Graphics and Woodwork. I liked it, I just wanted to do Art and Home Ec more than I wanted to do Woodwork. Because I knew this year we'd be doing sewing and that's something I wanted to do and I love cooking as well.

Girl: I dropped Woodwork and Music. I really liked Woodwork but my parents wanted me to do Business Studies. Yeah, they said it would probably be more useful. (Female students not taking technological subjects, Downend, low take-up, community/comprehensive)

In sum, students mainly relied on informal sources of advice (such as parents, siblings and friends) in making decisions about their subject choices. Parents were the most frequently mentioned source of advice, even where students chose to ignore such advice. The following section looks in further detail at the factors influencing girls' decisions regarding the take-up of traditionally male technological subjects.

6.5 GENDER DIFFERENCES IN THE TAKE-UP OF TECHNOLOGICAL SUBJECTS

Many of the students, both male and female, in the case-study schools viewed gender differences in the take-up of the traditionally male technological subjects as reflecting underlying differences in interest in particular subjects:

> Girl: Girls didn't opt for Woodwork, not many anyway. So it's not just guys who think it's a guys' subject, I think, I think it's both. (Female students taking technological subjects, Downend, low take-up, community/comprehensive)

A number of male students contrasted boys' "natural" affinity for the technological subjects with girls' preference for "female" subjects such as Home Economics:

> Boy: Girls tend to be moany and all that. They wouldn't really be interested in Woodwork as much as boys would, the same way I wouldn't be interested in Home Economics. I don't really like cooking and all that and girls, they want to be in groups, they want to be with girls on their own. I don't know really but boys, it's different, it's the same thing, boys and girls, girls don't really like doing boys' subjects and boys don't really like doing girls' subjects. (Male students, Clonmacken St., low take-up, community/comprehensive)

> Boy: [Boys are] more into it [technological subjects].

> Boy: Girls would be a bit afraid to do stuff.

> Boy: And cooking they'd rather.

> Boy: Do their nails.

> Boy: Housework and stuff. (Male students, Southmead, high take-up, community/comprehensive)

"Male" subjects were negatively labelled by some female students as "dirty", involving physical labour and working with machinery:

> Interviewer: Can I ask why did you not choose [technological subjects]?

> Girl: In case I'd get a splinter or something in Woodwork and I think they're more boys' things than girls. (Female students not

taking technological subjects, Clonmacken St., low take-up, community/comprehensive)

Girl: Because lads work with their hands more whereas we prefer more business, accounting and that.

Girl: They probably want to be like engineers or something because that's more of a man's job.

Girl: Girls are not interested in working with the machinery and everything.

Girl: Girls would rather do something that they could use for the future.

Girl: [We] don't want to get our hands dirty.

Girl: Break a nail or something. (Female students, Longwell Green, high take-up, vocational)

In contrast, some of the male students mentioned working with machinery as a positive feature of subjects such as Metalwork.

Some students differentiated among the technological subjects in terms of their perceived "suitability" for female students:

Girl: Most girls would be more into drawing [Technical Graphics] than they would be into doing shelves. (Female students taking technological subjects, Oldham Way, high take-up in TG and MT, coed secondary)

Boy: I think they'd [girls] be better at doing Tech Graphics . . . because they're usually neater when they write. (Male students, Downend, low take-up, community/comprehensive)

In many cases, gender stereotyping in relation to school subjects was linked to the labelling of related occupational areas with masculine identity embedded in the choice of particular occupations:

Girl: I'd say the lads would probably go for a real messy job. If they're getting an apprenticeship, they'd probably want something like a plumber or something really, really dirty that a girl wouldn't go near or something that yeah I'm a man, kind of

prove that. (Female students taking Technical Graphics, Oldham
Way, high take-up in TG and MT, coed secondary)

This was seen as analogous to the link between sports and gender identities in the school setting:

Girl: Sports is good, some of us play with the boys and they're
kind of like it's a boys' sport, we don't want you on it.

Girl: Like soccer or something like that.

Girl: Yeah, because we've just started a soccer team and they're
all like it's a man's sport, go back to basketball. (Female students
taking Technical Graphics, Oldham Way, high take-up in TG and
MT, coed secondary)

Existing gendered patterns of take-up could become self-perpetuating
within schools as students were reluctant to stand out from the crowd in
choosing non-traditional subjects:

I think loads of girls wanted to do Metalwork but they were afraid
to because all the other girls were doing Geography. (Male students, Glenveagh Road, low take-up, vocational)

However, some girls reported that being in a predominantly male class
was actually a motivation for taking technological subjects:

Interviewer: Why did you pick Woodwork?

Girl: Because that was the only chance to mix with boys, there
was no other chance we had to mix. (Female students, Glenveagh
Road, low take-up, vocational)

Another group saw male-dominated classes as having a better atmosphere:

Girl: I don't mind being in a class with the boys, I'd rather be in
classes with boys than I would be with girls.

Girl: You get more a better laugh.

Girl: You get along with the boys.

Girl: They're not as bitchy.

Girl: Better laugh as well. (Female students taking Materials Technology, Oldham Way, high take-up, coed secondary)

Male students were mixed in their views about the female students who took technological subjects. One group felt that female students were not "able" to take these subjects:

Boy: The girls weren't really able to do Metalwork.

Boy: [The girls] weren't very good.

Boy: They got all sweaty and all.

Boy: Only one girl came and she just left. (Male students, Glenveagh Road, low take-up, vocational)

However, this group did object to the school's decision to allocate places mainly to boys when Metalwork was over-subscribed and had relatively neutral attitudes to the girls taking Materials Technology ("they just hang out with us").

Another group of boys felt the (individual) girls who took Metalwork were not particularly interested in the subject for its own sake:

Interviewer: What about Metalwork?

Boy: [There are] two girls in that class.

Boy: They do nothing but mess.

Interviewer: Are they getting on okay?

Boy: No.

Boy: They just laugh.

Boy: The lads that are in that class they're all interested in Metalwork but the girls aren't.

Interviewer: Why are they there in the first place then?

Boy: They don't want to do . . . . Business Studies.

Boy: One of the girls was fine until the other one came . . . and they just started messing

Boy: Yeah, they're messing. The only reason they were doing Metalwork is because they're trying to be with their friends and all. They are both friends. (Male students, Longwell Green, high take-up, vocational)

However, their views appeared to be related to the particular students involved as the male students described a female student in another practical subject as being the "best in the class" (male students, Longwell Green). In contrast, two other groups of boys had neutral, if not positive, views about girls taking technological subjects, although interestingly one student chose to express these views in quite gendered terms:

Interviewer: What do you think of the girls who have chosen Metalwork or Technical Graphics?

Boy: Fair play to them.

Boy: Fair play to them, yeah.

Boy: At least they're trying it out.

Boy: They're man enough to do it. (Male students, Southmead, high take-up, community/comprehensive)

Interviewer: What do you think of girls doing Metalwork or girls doing Woodwork?

Boy: There's nothing wrong with it.

Boy: Don't mind it. (Male students, Churchwood, high take-up, vocational)

In spite of the relatively neutral views among the latter group regarding girls taking technological subjects, the boys tended to report that female students did not do as well in Metalwork as male students due to their lack of physical strength. However, in the course of the discussion, they moderated their view and asserted that it related to "some" female students only:

Interviewer: So do you think that the girls are better than boys in Metalwork?

Boy: No.

Boy: A good bit behind.

Interviewer: Why is that?

Boy: We're quicker.

Boy: Stronger.

Boy: More strength.

Boy: More strength yeah for filing and stuff.

Boy: Cutting through it [metal].

Boy: Bending and that.

Interviewer: So you think that girls are not strong enough for Metalwork?

Boy: Some girls are.

Boy: Some of them are too slow. (Male students, Churchwood, high take-up, vocational)

A similar pattern emerged in Oldham Way where male students described female students in their Materials Technology class as "alright" but "not as good" at the subject as the boys. One boy in this group asserted that "girls should stick to their cooking".

Two groups of female students taking technological subjects reported negative attitudes to them on the part of boys in their class:

Interviewer: Is there anything about Woodwork you don't like?

Girl: The guys.

Interviewer: Why?

Girl: They think they're so great, they think they're all like oh girls can't do Woodwork, even though we get higher grades than them, they're very chauvinistic about it. (Female students taking technological subjects, Downend, low take-up, community/ comprehensive)

Some female students in Glenveagh Road also reported being "jeered" by male students in their Materials Technology. However, one girl in

Downend school who was the only one in a class of boys taking a practical subject reported that "they [the boys] treat me like one of themselves really".

Students' perceptions of teacher attitudes to girls taking non-traditional subjects were similarly mixed. Two groups of students reported stereotyped views among some teachers:

> Interviewer: Is there anything you don't like about the subject?
>
> Girl: No, the teacher a bit, you get a hard time because you're the only girl.
>
> . . .
>
> Girl: The boys do be around our desk and he thinks if they don't do the work, it's my fault, that I'm disrupting their work. (Female students taking technological subjects, Riversdale Lane, low take-up, vocational)
>
> Girl: Because some teachers think why would you want to do Metalwork, [it's] going to do nothing for you.
>
> Girl: The Geography teacher said we're not tomboys, we shouldn't be doing Metalwork, we should be doing Geography. (Female students not taking technological subjects, Glenveagh Road, low take-up, vocational)

However, another group of students felt that teachers of technological subjects did not treat female and male students differently:

> Interviewer: Do you think that there is a difference [in] how teachers get on with boys and girls [in practical subject classes]?
>
> Girl: I think it's the same.
>
> Girl: He treats us all equally.
>
> Girl: No, he hasn't got a favourite, it's just everyone is the same. (Female students taking technological subjects, Oldham Way, high take-up, coed secondary)

In some cases, male teachers of technological subjects were even seen as being "always nice to the girls" (female students, Downend) and as being more lenient with female students ("he lets us off with everything", female students, Oldham Way).

Some gender stereotyping was evident among at least some students across all of the case-study schools when talking to the students about subject choice and future careers. However, some students more actively challenged stereotyping in subject and occupational arenas:

> Boy: [Girls] could do all the same things like being an architect. It's not like just because you're a girl and you're doing Metalwork or Woodwork that you're not going to get a job.

> Boy: People are hiring you for doing Metalwork and for doing Woodwork. I don't think they should care really what sex you are, male or female, as long as you know how to do the job.

> Boy: I think a woman can do a better job than a male can do. (Male students, Longwell Green, high take-up, vocational)

> Girl: But there's nothing to say that it's [Woodwork] a guys' subject in any way.

> Girl: Whoever got that idea I don't know where they got it from. (Female students taking technological subjects, Downend, low take-up, community/comprehensive)

An interesting contrast emerges when students were asked about their perceptions of boys taking a non-traditional subject, namely, Home Economics[11]. Gender stereotyping was evident among some male students who regarded the subject as suitable (only) for girls:

> Boy: [B]oys doing Home Ec, there's something wrong with that.

> Boy: We're not going to want to sew or something. (Male students, Churchwood, high take-up, vocational)

> Boy: Sure isn't it all about pregnancy and everything as well, boys would be no good at that I'd say. (Male students, Downend, low take-up, community/comprehensive)

---

[11] All of the schools participating in the study provided Home Economics.

Boy: You'd never see boys cooking.

Boy: It's the woman's job to cook in the house.

Boy: Yeah to clean houses. (Male students, Oakleaf Ave, low take-up, vocational)

Some of the female students also invoked gender stereotypes in considering that boys would potentially be "clumsy and stuff" and "a pack of messers" in Home Economics class (Mountainview St., non-provision, girls' secondary) and would find the subject more difficult ("they struggle trying to cook and sew", Oakleaf Ave, low take-up, vocational). However, such views were challenged by some other students:

Girl: And Home Economics is more so for girls.

Girl: Because you've the cooking and cleaning stuff.

Girl: But lads can still cook, just because they're boys it doesn't mean they can't cook and girls can still do Woodwork as well. (Mountainview St., non-provision, girls' secondary)

Indeed, a few students in Southmead and Oldham Way schools mentioned fear of ridicule and of being the only boy in a class of girls as reasons for not choosing the subject. One group of girls asserted that boys taking Home Economics were more likely to be mocked by other boys but not by girls:

Girl: It's not really girls that would mind, it's the boys, they would all tease them.

Girl: Yeah, the boys would jeer.

. . .

Girl: It would be a bit weird to see a boy in a class that mostly girls do but it wouldn't be that bad, it would be the lads that would pick on the boys. (Female students, Churchwood, high take-up, vocational)

Girl: I think it's the people that don't take the class, they think it's a real girlie subject and they'll say to the ones that do . . . old man

> sitting at home in a rocking chair knitting. (Female students, Downend, low take-up, community/comprehensive)

However, many other students reported that male students were as good at the subject as their female counterparts:

> Boy: Girls are meant to be better at it. I think loads of boys are deadly at it, like at cooking. (Male students, Greenbank, non-provision, coed secondary)

> Girl: The boys like doing the cooking as well, they're more into the cooking and they're all doing really well, they're all trying really hard on their cushions.

> Girl: There's this lad in our class . . . and he's better at doing the stitching than I am. (Female students, Longwell Green, high take-up, vocational)

These students did not feel that others had a particular problem with boys taking the subject:

> Boy: [Y]our class is doing it and it's only your class in it so it doesn't really get talked about that much about males doing home economics or sewing or anything in our class anyway. (Male students, Longwell Green, high take-up, vocational)

> Girl: No one bothers really, if he says that he has Home Ec, it's just alright I have wood I'll see you later, it's not a big problem, its just another class. (Oldham Way, high take-up in TG and MT, coed secondary)

Overall, gender stereotyping was evident in relation to the views of many students regarding Technical Graphics, Materials Technology (Wood) and, perhaps most markedly, Metalwork. However, the labelling of these subjects as "male" was contested by some students and ambiguities were evident in how male students regarded female students who selected such subjects. A similar pattern was evident in relation to the traditionally female subject of Home Economics, with stereotyping evident among some groups of students but other students challenging such preconceptions.

6.6 CONCLUSIONS

Students in the case-study schools tended to rely primarily on informal sources of advice, especially their parents, in making decisions about which subjects to select at junior cycle. In many ways, student choice was subject to constraints: some schools allowed a limited selection of subject options while students in five of the schools were not always allocated the subjects they selected. There was a certain degree of dissatisfaction among some students about constraints on their choices and a number were unhappy with the subjects they were taking for the Junior Certificate.

A more active and hands-on approach to learning was a motivating factor for both male and female students in selecting technological subjects at junior cycle level. However, these subjects tended to be labelled as "male" because of their perceived reliance on physical strength and the "dirty" work involved. There were a number of contradictions involved in students' perceptions of these subjects. Some male students reported "no problem" with girls taking the technological subjects but often highlighted boys' natural superiority in these subjects. Furthermore, some female students considered in theory that all students should have access to technological subjects but felt that these subjects were "not for them" at a personal level. In contrast, existing gender stereotypes were challenged by some students, both male and female.

Chapter Seven

CHANGES IN THE SYLLABI OF TECHNOLOGICAL SUBJECTS: IMPLICATIONS FOR GENDER DIFFERENCES IN TAKE-UP

7.1 INTRODUCTION

Drawing on in-depth interviews with the teachers of Materials Technology (Wood), Metalwork and Technical Graphics, this chapter explores teacher views on a range of issues relating to teaching technological subjects at junior cycle level. In particular, it discusses changes that have taken place in the syllabi and the implications these changes may have for gender differences take-up of technological subjects. Other topics addressed in this chapter relate to approaches taken to teaching technological subjects and homework given to the students. In total, nineteen subject teachers of Materials Technology (Wood), Metalwork and Technical Graphics were interviewed for the study. The chapter supplements teacher perspectives with students' views on teaching methods and homework in the technological subjects. The following section focuses specifically on issues related to gender and subject content. The next section discusses the perceived suitability of the technical subjects for different academic ability levels. The fourth section deals with methods used in teaching the technological subjects.

7.2 GENDER AND SUBJECT CONTENT

Previous chapters have examined the strongly gendered perceptions of technological subjects among students. The gender stereotyping evident from the interviews with subject teachers and students can be seen in the context of cultural and structural reproduction of certain attitudes in a society as well as with dispositions enforced by social structures including schools (see Harris, 1979). Traditionally Materials Technology (Wood), Metalwork and Technical Graphics were perceived to be "male" subjects involving working with heavy materials and machinery in a "workshop" setting. This image of classrooms of some technological subjects as "workshops" have been persistent and contribute to gendered perceptions of these subjects. However, over recent decades the syllabi of technological subjects have undergone revision, with an increased focus on projects and design rather than making abstract items, which the students in the past perceived to have little relevance:

> the kids used to say we're making a nothing, because it was nothing, just four pieces joined together and very difficult but there was actually no shape, didn't mean anything to them, at least now it means something, there's a relevance there. (Glenveagh Road, low take-up in TG and MT, vocational).

In addition, in many cases students were using heavy material in their classes:

> There was a time if you go back into the dark ages when I was in school, we would have metal which would be six millimetre thick steel and that's what you were cutting and filing and it was heavy, hard work (Churchwood, high take-up, vocational, Principal).

Changes in the content of the technological subjects and different materials used were highlighted by other subject teachers: in Metalwork, the materials have become lighter and the subject also has a project-based approach:

> Now they have sheet material and it wouldn't be any more than half a millimetre thick and there's a lot of plastic and a lot of Perspex and non-ferrous metals and the projects themselves are nice dainty little projects, could be aeroplanes, helicopters for the Junior Cert programme. (Churchwood, high take-up, vocational)

> The projects are . . . there is an end product and there's so much design and you can incorporate jewellery, enamelling, piercing,

> metalwork is so broad now, there's so many processes, you don't
> have to make, it just doesn't have to be riveting and hammering
> and filing with one big piece of black . . . steel or something, you
> can introduce so many different things now. (Southmead, high
> take-up, community/comprehensive)

Considering these changes, a number of teachers observed that the new
syllabi are more suitable for girls than in the past as the tasks are more
focused on design rather than skills-based practical work demanding
physical strength. There has been a move away from using heavier materials with the result that the subjects were now seen as more "girl-
friendly":

> Interviewer: So you're generally quite satisfied with the syllabus?
>
> MT Teacher: As far as gender goes, yes, I think it couldn't be any
> better than it is. . . . [The design element] was never there before
> in the old syllabus, it's changed a lot and it's very amenable for
> girls. (Oakleaf Ave., low take-up, vocational)
>
> I think now even with the projects that are being made, [Metal-
> work] . . . it's friendlier to girls and even to the smaller male stu-
> dents. (Churchwood, high take-up, vocational)

However, these changes were not seen as sufficient to alter the strong
gender stereotyping associated with the subjects (see Chapters Five and
Six). A teacher in Oakleaf Avenue vocational school considered that
broader changes were needed in people's perceptions in order to make
the subject more attractive to female students, an issue discussed in the
earlier chapters:

> If there was something that could be done to make [Metalwork]
> more attractive for girls, I think it's probably a much bigger ques-
> tion and problem than just changing the syllabus. (Oakleaf Ave.,
> low take-up, vocational)

This section discussed how technological subjects are now, in principle,
more accessible for both sexes, due to the changed foci of the syllabi as
well as using lighter materials in the class. How subject teachers perceive

the suitability of their subject to different ability levels is explored in the following section.

7.3 ACADEMIC ABILITY LEVELS IN MATERIALS TECHNOLOGY (WOOD), METALWORK AND TECHNICAL GRAPHICS

A number of authors have discussed the availability of certain subjects to different ability groups (see Oakes, 1990). She reports that lower track students are often excluded from taking subjects such as advanced Science and Math courses. This indicates schools' decision in what kind of knowledge is deemed suitable to different subject groups. Subjects with a stronger technological component have frequently been targeted towards lower ability students, particularly boys. In order to explore the perceived suitability of technological subjects for different ability groups in Ireland, subject teachers in the three technological subjects reviewed in this study were interviewed. In general, the teachers observed that, while broadly satisfied with the suitability of the syllabi in the three technological subjects for Junior Certificate students, there are also some problem areas. In particular, less academically able students were found to have difficulty in coping with the theoretical components of the syllabi. In addition, students with lower levels of self-confidence were seen as experiencing difficulties. These ideas are expressed in an interview with a teacher of Materials Technology (Wood) in Longwell Green vocational school. He reported that lower ability students find it hard to come up with ideas for projects and have lower confidence levels compared to other students:

> And it's even to get [some students] to develop their own ideas, particularly as I say with the weaker ones, a lot of them they're very easily led but they don't have the confidence or maybe they don't have the ability or maybe they just don't have the know how or the get up and go to go and do it themselves. [. . .] You know results, I know they're very important but they're very important relative to where you're going to go and if you've a weak student and if they achieve something and they're happy enough with that, I think that they've got a service the same as anybody else. (MT teacher, Longwell Green, high take-up, vocational)

The importance of the feeling of accomplishment on completion of a project for less academic students was also stressed by other teachers of technological subjects. In order to encourage the feeling of accomplishment and "empower" the students, in some cases, weaker students were encouraged to work at their own pace:

> I would mainly just let them [less academic students] work to their own level [in Metalwork classes], just as long as . . . they're not just sitting doing nothing. . . . I wouldn't hold that against the ones that are behind, I'd say this is the project and this is what we get done. (Churchwood, high take-up, vocational)

A number of teachers of Technical Graphics commented on difficulties with the syllabus for certain groups of students. A teacher in Glenveagh Road vocational school argued that less academically able students find it difficult to cope with the theory component of the syllabus, as it requires a good literacy level:

> The big obstacle to the syllabus is the theoretical part of the syllabus [in Technical Graphics]. It is based very much on having a good command of the English language, I don't think it considers the poor ability of an awful lot of students (TG Teacher, Glenveagh Road, low take-up in TG and MT, vocational)

Another criticism centred on the assessment mode for students taking the subject at ordinary level, which was not considered challenging enough for higher ability students while weaker students would not be able to cope with anything more complicated:

> . . . particularly the theoretical course at pass level is very much ticking boxes and some people think that's great but I think it's a disaster because students just get into the habit of just ticking, there's no mental exercising at all and it could be much more like the Leaving Cert Applied where it will ask the question and then there's an area for them to fill it in and it's much more, the students can impart their knowledge, they have the knowledge but the weak students can't go along and do it, I'd see that as a big barrier. (Glenveagh Road, low take-up in TG and MT, vocational)

The syllabus at Junior Certificate higher level was considered by many teachers to be significantly more difficult than that at ordinary level with a large gap in requirements between the two levels. In addition, less academically able students were perceived to have difficulties with being able to visualise what they need to produce for Technical Graphics classes:

> I'd say at Junior Cert level Technical Graphics, ordinary level [is] very easy to get through but you've got to learn certain techniques and you've got to be able to . . . be able to visualise things. At honours level in Junior Cert it's nearly as difficult, I'd say certain questions as pass Leaving Cert and it is very difficult for some kids to be able to visualise, especially the weaker students, what something is going to look like. . . . There is such a difference between the ordinary level and the higher level [in Technical Graphics], I'd have a few students now who are doing ordinary level, who probably wouldn't make the higher level but if it was a little bit easier they'd have a shot at it and they might pass and it would be far better for them for their own self esteem, that's the only quibble I have with it. There's such a massive difference that if somebody who is a little bit less than average, can't make the jump. (Churchwood, high take-up, vocational)

The fact that there is no direct "outcome" at the end of the process compared to Materials Technology and Metalwork was also seen to pose problems for some students:

> . . . the fact that it's not seen that you're making stuff and you're not bringing something home. Most weeks students I would have down in the Metalwork room would bring something home and they're able to say Ma look what I made and it's up on the mantelpiece and you've parents come in saying "Jesus will you stop letting them make those things" (Churchwood, high take-up, vocational).

In the same vein, difficulties with the Technical Graphics syllabus were discussed by a teacher in Oakleaf Avenue vocational school who also considered the syllabus unsuitable for less able students. He argued that sustaining students' interest in the subject becomes difficult as the subject involves a considerable mathematical component. Time constraints were seen as preventing teachers using materials and tasks that could be more suitable for such students. Having students of mixed ability levels in the same classroom was seen to pose additional problems, as a teacher is required to consider the needs of all students:

> Interviewer: Is the syllabus suitable for all abilities?
>
> TG Teacher: Well it probably isn't, no, its ok for the higher level, the lower level it's very difficult to keep them interested and enjoying it because again they've an examination to pass and so it's tough for them. It's not the best subject for them, it's only a graphical form of mathematics really and so it's not always the most interesting. Whereas there are things that aren't in the syllabus that could be interesting but you don't get time to do it and again the problem is there's no streaming, which means I'm teaching two different levels in the one class all the time. (Oakleaf Ave., low take-up, vocational)
>
> [The syllabus works] providing the class number is small, I don't mean a one to one but say perhaps a teacher to every 5, 6, 7 maybe but not 1 to 20. . . . Because it's very difficult to get around the class and it's very difficult to instil confidence in the students because even within 20, lower ability students you have further divides there, further levels. The weaker the students are the smaller the groups, it's a preference. (TG teacher, Longwell Green, high take-up, vocational)

The difficulty of learning Technical Graphics in a mixed ability context was also mentioned by one of the students:

> Girl: It [the Technical Graphics lesson] kind of goes slow, I know you have to wait, if you know something and then there's someone else who doesn't, it kind of gets annoying because you're waiting for ages until they get it right. I know it's not their fault but it kind of goes really slow. (Oldham Way, high take-up in TG and MT, coed secondary)

In sum, some aspects of the Materials Technology (Wood) and Metalwork syllabi were seen as difficult for less academically able students, particularly the requirement to come up with an original design and the theory component of the course. However, these subjects were also seen as providing a sense of accomplishment to students who may not achieve highly in the more "academic" subjects (see Riddell, 1992). Compared to Materials Technology and Metalwork, Technical Graphics was seen as more difficult for certain students, particularly at higher level.

7.4 APPROACHES TO TEACHING TECHNOLOGICAL SUBJECTS

This section explores teaching techniques and approaches used by teachers of Materials Technology (Wood), Metalwork and Technical Graphics in the case-study schools. Although perceived by students as "practically orientated subjects", Materials Technology (Wood), Metalwork and Technical Graphics also have a theoretical component. Engaging students in learning theory, however, is often seen as a major task in all three subjects:

> One major problem I have in Woodwork is that the kids do not want to do theory, it is a major problem always and if I could do anything I'd nearly scrap the theory because it makes life hell down there (Churchwood, high take-up, vocational).

In all of the case-study schools, teachers reported that students in their classes were not as interested in the theoretical component of the subject. According to them, the students perceive these classes as a "break" from general classes such as English and Mathematics. Coming to class is seen as doing "something practical" and having a certain degree of freedom to move around and talk to other students rather than working from textbooks:

> They [students] feel we're coming down now, we can do practical work, we're walking around the benches, we're drilling timber, we're marking out and I want them to put all that away and get out books and start writing and they don't want to do that, they feel Woodwork is not for that, Woodwork is for doing woodwork. And if they've had six general classes all day and they come down to me, obviously they don't want another gen-

eral class, so it does make it difficult. (Churchwood, high take-up, vocational).

Addressing this difficulty, presenting theoretical material for students was sometimes done using handouts and printouts rather than students taking notes in class in order to make it more interesting. In order to sustain students' interest, many teachers of Technical graphics now use computers in their classes. The importance of good textbooks was also highlighted by several teachers.

> Well with all handouts and printouts now in theory, theory [in Woodwork] has become easier than in years gone by when they had to write everything. Now you can give them a handout and they can learn the questions and learn all about the structure of wood and seasoning and that and then we have a good textbook, which we hadn't 30 years ago, so that area has improved a lot. (Riversdale Lane, low take-up, vocational)

> You'd be covering all the different things [in Technical Graphics] . . . course work really and they'd be doing a lot of board drawing and a small little bit of computer-aided drawing, just to give them a feel for it. They prefer [working with the computer] now to the board drawing, which is the way drawing is going to go, well I feel anyway, it's the way it's heading. Follow the syllabus, try and cover it all so that they have a choice of topics in their exam. (Clonmacken St., low take-up in TG and MT, community/comprehensive)

Some teachers prefer to keep theory and practice classes separate. However, a certain amount of theory is often presented during the practical classes combined with working on the project:

> I don't mix the two [theory and practice]. I mean obviously there's explanations as to why we do things and how we do things, that's all theory if you like but they're doing it, but then we'll get the theory classes. Even when we're dealing with timber I'd be explaining the differences with the timber when I'm giving them the wood, how some are easier to work and some react dif-

ferently to others. But then we do a theory class [in Woodwork]
as well. (Oakleaf Ave., low take-up, vocational)

In general, the coverage of theory increases from first to third year (see
below):

I do all practical work in the first year, I cover quite a lot of the
practical ground and then in second year I do a lot of theory with
a small bit of practical and then in third year a combination of the
[two] until Christmas and then they get their design brief and they
take it from there then on their own. Again that is another area
that's a problem because, once they get the design brief, theory
[in Metalwork] is out the door. (Glenveagh Road, low take-up in
TG and MT, vocational)

Compared to Materials Technology (Wood) and Metalwork, teaching
approaches in Technical Graphics were seen as involving a greater emphasis on problem-solving exercises. The practical and theory components within the subject were seen as more strongly linked than in the
other two subjects with a strong emphasis on the hands-on aspect of the
course:

Well, in the drawing basically it's all practical work, you're actually drawing and problem solving. A certain amount of theory is
involved in the practical solving, the nature of drawing, technical
graphics. There would be a few things but they're generally written down as text on a sheet that they would be working on. (Riversdale Lane, low take-up, vocational)

Not surprisingly, some teachers felt that more academically able students
are better at coping with the theory component than less able students
(see Section 7.3):

There would be students who would be more academic, they
would be better at theory, pass Junior Cert students, they would
have reading difficulties and obviously writing difficulties,
they're not going to do very well on the written part, they're not
going to do as well as they are on the practical part and that
would apply to both boys and girls, I would imagine. (Clon-

macken St., low take-up in TG and MT, community/compre-
hensive)

In general, students work on their own during the classes with each student working on their individual project. However, in most cases certain
interaction with other students is allowed in class, something that all students enjoy:

> [The students in Woodwork classes] would be doing it on their
> own, the idea is that they would make a project which they could
> then take home [. . .] we would get them to do an individual project
> which they can then bring home and show the parents. This is the
> type of thing I've been working on and we find it very good for
> their motivation, they're so proud when they actually complete
> something and they get to bring it home for the first time. So that's
> the main reason why we shied away from doing group work or do-
> ing joint projects because then the whole issue well whose is it, do
> they bring it home or is it just something that gets left in the school.
> (Downend, low take-up, community/comprehensive)

In general, students are allowed more freedom to ask assistance from
other students and to walk around compared to academic subject classes:

> [Students work] on their own, but obviously we'd encourage co-
> operation. . . . They've plenty of latitude to talk to whomever they
> want or ask questions or whatever they want, no problem. (Oak-
> leaf Avenue, low take-up, vocational)

> They work individually [in Technical Graphics], each student has
> his own desk, you would have a maximum of 24 in the room and
> you would have 24 drawing desks, each individual with his own
> set-up. They work individually in so far as they work at their own
> desk but they are within a group, ok you have two desks together
> as such but each individual, there is flexibility to move around
> and see. (Riversdale Lane, low take-up, vocational)

Group work was not considered to be an option by some subject teachers. In some cases it was considered difficult because of large class sizes:

> Group work [in Metalwork] is very hard in a big class as such I
> find, because you might have one or two students who would get
> lazy and another two might end up doing all the work with them.
> (Churchwood, high take-up, vocational)

As discussed in earlier sections, the syllabi of the technological subjects
are now design- and project-based and more accessible for different
groups of students. The approach taken in most cases is to identify a project, design it and finally produce an object students have chosen as their
project.

> Well we pick some project we want to make and I usually try and
> get them to draw out drawings of the project, the way they see the
> project and ideally we will put all those together and then design
> the project from that, . . . I'll generally keep an eye on what
> they're doing. And we'll work our way through the project.
> (Churchwood, high take-up, vocational)

This indicates a shift in emphasis from the past whereby the work was
more abstract and demanded greater physical strength. It can be argued
that the new approach enables a wider variety of students to enjoy the
subject. Certain similarities can be identified between the approaches
used in all three subjects. In all cases during first year, classes are more
structured and focus on introducing students to the basic skills including
the use of tools, basic elements of safety and simpler projects. Subsequent year groups are presented with an increasing amount of theory and
involve preparation for the Junior Certificate exam:

> In first year it's really well structured in that you would have a
> number of different tasks or projects that would cover the basic
> skills, using tools and so on and safety and getting familiar with
> drawing and so on. (Southmead, high take-up, community/
> comprehensive)

Student Perceptions of Subject Content

Groups of second year students were asked how they felt about the theory component in their technological classes. In keeping with teacher
perceptions, the majority preferred the practical component to the theory

which they found boring, repetitive and not always well presented by the subject teacher:

> Girl: [Materials Technology (Wood) is] Oh just boring.
>
> Interviewer: What do you find boring?
>
> Girl: Learning about nails and stuff.
>
> Girl: Where does bits of wood come from, what part of the tree.
>
> Girl: Yeah exactly.
>
> Girl: He's gone over different types of nails three times in a row. (Female students taking Materials Technology, Downend, low take-up, community/comprehensive)

> Girl: Yeah, it's grand in them classes but the theory...
>
> Girl: [Theory] kind of goes on a bit. (Female students taking Materials Technology, Longwell Green, high take-up, vocational)

> Girl: It's good when you're making things . . . but not the theory. (Female students taking technological subjects, Southmead, high take-up, community/comprehensive)

> Boy: [I would] Rather be active [in MT class] than having to sit down and just listen. (Male students, Churchwood, high take-up, vocational)

> Boy: I like doing practical in Metalwork but I don't like doing the theory, I hate doing theory. When he does the theory all he does is shouts.
>
> Boy: Shout at everybody
>
> Boy: Very annoying. (Male students, Glenveagh Road, low take-up in TG and MT, medium take-up in MW, vocational)

In keeping with teacher reports, students mentioned that they covered less theory in second year:

> Girl: Mainly this year we've been doing, we haven't done so much theory because you do most of your theory in third year, at

the start of third year before you get what you're supposed to do for the actual Junior Cert. (Female students taking technological subjects, Downend, low take-up, community/comprehensive)

Interviewer: What do you think of the theory in Technical Graphics?

Boy: We don't really do much, he gives us one topic.

Boy: Yeah, he just tells us to do it.

Boy: He gives us a topic and he'll talk about it for a few minutes in class and then we'll spend the rest of the class drawing. (Male students, Longwell Green, high take-up, vocational)

The students were also asked whether they worked independently or in groups in their practical classes. As already indicated by the subject teachers, there is a certain amount of interaction during the classes between students. However, not all teachers seem to exercise similar flexibility with their students:

Interviewer: Do you work on your own or in a group?

Girl: We work on our own but then if we don't know something either ask the teacher or ask someone beside us.

Girl: We usually get in trouble if we ask someone beside us. (Female students taking Technical Graphics, Oldham Way, high take-up, coed secondary)

Interviewer: Do you work mostly on your own or with a friend?

Boy: Well we each do our own project but we can talk to each other and help each other. (Male students, Oakleaf Ave., low take-up, vocational)

Interviewer: Do you work mostly on your own or as a group or in pairs?

Boy: On your own basically, you'd turn around and ask the other person how to do this and that. (Male students, Clonmacken St., low take-up, community/comprehensive)

Interviewer: So what are Metalwork classes like?

Boy: They're all right.

Interviewer: What do you do?

Boy: Walk around.

Boy: Walk around, have a chat . . . we do work sometimes. (Male students, Oakleaf Ave., low take-up, vocational)

Homework in the Technological Subjects

The amount of homework is often an issue for junior cycle students, especially for those in lower ability groups. One study of teachers of first year students (Smyth, et al., 2004) indicated that students were likely to get less regular homework in the technological subjects than in some other subject areas. This section investigates whether teachers give regular homework to their second year students in Materials Technology (Wood), Metalwork and Technical Graphics. Compared to more "academic" subjects (such as Maths), the amount of homework given in all three technological subjects tends to be limited and focuses on revision of material covered in the class and/or the theoretical component of the course.

> I don't give a lot of homework because I can cover the syllabus and they can get good marks very easily, they do have to do some homework yeah but not an awful lot. (Oakleaf Ave., low take-up, vocational)

> We don't give homework in Woodwork because again we made the decision not to ask them to buy a text book in first year because we felt it was unfair to ask them to pay maybe €15 or €20 for a text book that they may not actually use beyond first year, if they decide not to keep a subject up. So what we actually decided was that we have a class set of books that we use with the first years for teaching theory, what little we do of it but we actually wait until second year until they've actually opted for the subject before we ask them to get a text book. (Downend, low take-up, community/comprehensive)

Only a few Materials Technology (Wood) teachers reported giving regular homework to their students:

> I do, in homework I would try and get them to do a reasonable amount of homework in theory in particular, sometimes the students take home bits and pieces of their woodwork and if they have facilities at home and they have the interest they do actually work on them at home. (Southmead, high take-up, community/comprehensive)

> Interviewer: Would you give homework?

> Teacher: Sometimes, but the ability of the student in the school has kind of dropped so it's quite hard, there's not a culture there of homework so it's frustrating at times, the homework doesn't come back. (Glenveagh Road, low take-up in TG and MT, medium take-up in MW, vocational)

Some homework comprises bringing certain materials to school that could be used in class rather than formal written work:

> Yes [I give homework] only once a week, it's not like other subjects, some of them don't look on it as homework when you ask them to bring in five nails or five screws or five leads, they don't see that as homework but it is actual homework from my side. (Riversdale Lane, low take-up, vocational)

However, teachers often expected students to revise material, especially theoretical material, after school:

> When I say I don't give them homework, we do theory, their homework would be go back over what we have done, their homework from practical would be you have a theory book, if there's anything you're not sure about, there's a book there, look at it, if you can't find the answer come back and ask me. I just find our time is so short that I physically wouldn't have the time to sit down and expect 20 or 24 kids to come up to me with a copy, it doesn't lend itself in a major way to homework I suppose [. . .] but homework, even though I expect that they will be using their theory book, I'm not going to call around to their houses,

> I'm not going to spend half the day arguing why didn't you learn it last night because there's so many others in the class who want to get on with the work. (Longwell Green, high take-up, vocational)

> I give them homework but it's often reading or to revise, rather than literally written homework, they feel Woodwork is not for homework, again it's practical work, they feel they want to do practical work only, they don't want to do their write ups, they don't want to do theory, so the theory is a constant battle with the class. (Churchwood, high take-up, vocational)

A number of teachers give homework to their Metalwork classes. As in Materials Technology, this mostly covers the revision of theory:

> Yes, [I am] constantly giving them homework, not as much this year now because I'm very busy myself, I would do it once a week now. (Riversdale Lane, low take-up, vocational)

> Yeah, they get [homework], supposing we were at drawings or note taking and one period of 35 minutes is very short and you're running out of time so they have a reference text book, so they go back, research the text book and fill in their own notes opposite the diagrams. (Longwell Green, high take-up, vocational)

Similarly to the other two technological subjects, homework in Technical Graphics tends to be based on material covered in the class. Students revise theory, do a drawing or finish work started in the class for their homework:

> Again for Technical Graphics they would have homework to do based on continuation of what they would have done in class. (Downend, low take-up, community/comprehensive)

> Well I use the workbook a lot and there's a lot of exercises in the workbook and then as I say we can start it in class, particularly single period classes and they carry it home. I give them the ideas on how they answer the questions and they take them home and they answer the questions and bring them back in and they're

checked and assessed. (Longwell Green, high take-up, vocational)

Interviewer: Do you give homework to your students in Technical Graphics?

Teacher: It's hard to do, yes I do when I can, I'm reluctant to give
it to first years for a while, I don't want to turn them off the subject. . . . I do do it with second year and definitely on into third
year, short questions coming up towards the exam but they don't
generally have the equipment at home to do a massive amount of
it. (Churchwood, high take-up, vocational)

Interviewer: Do you set homework in Woodwork and Technical
Graphics?

Teacher: Yes. If I were to implement a strict regime of getting
homework from students I would spend more time looking for it,
writing notes etc. I take the homework from the students who do
the homework. (Clonmacken St., low take-up, community/com-
prehensive)

Students' Perspectives on Homework

Second year students' perspectives on homework in Materials Technology (Wood), Metalwork and Technical Graphics were also investigated.
As discussed above, the extent to which they get regular homework in
these subjects varied. While some students reported getting a fair amount
of homework, others were given very little, if anything, to prepare at
home. Homework was not given every night so that students felt they
had enough time to prepare:

Boy: Very little, all we ever have to do is write a small report or
something. (Male students taking MT, Downend, low take-up,
community/comprehensive)

Girl: There's a fair amount to do for the report but we wouldn't
have homework every night, you'd have to have this due for then.
(Female students taking MT, Downend, low take-up, commu-
nity/comprehensive)

Boy: The only subjects we never get homework in are Woodwork and TG. (Male students, Longwell Green, high take-up, vocational)

Girl: It's usually to repeat the work that you done in class, probably get it once a week, if that, for Technical Graphics. (Female students, Oldham Way, high take-up, coed secondary)

Overall, there appeared to be less emphasis on giving formal homework to students in the technological subjects. However, students were expected by teachers to revise material, especially the theoretical components of the course, on an on-going basis. It could be argued that the "hands on" approach in technological subjects accompanied by a modest amount of homework may make these subjects especially suitable for less academically orientated students in providing them with a sense of achievement.

7.5 CONCLUSIONS

This chapter has indicated that changes in the syllabi towards a greater emphasis on design elements were seen as at least having the potential to attract more female students. In the case of Metalwork, the fact that students work with lighter metals was seen as decreasing the physical demands of the subject. In Technical Graphics, the introduction of computer-aided design was seen as being welcomed by both boys and girls. In terms of the suitability of technological subjects for different ability groups, teachers were somewhat mixed in their views about the desired balance between basic skills and design in these subjects. In particular, less academically able students were seen as struggling with certain aspects of the syllabi, especially the design component and theory, particularly in Technical Graphics.

All three technological subjects discussed in this study comprise theoretical as well as practical components. While theory is taught in separate classes in some cases, it is often integrated into students' work on a project. It is generally acknowledged that students have to be prepared for the theory paper in their Junior Certificate exam even if they are not seen as particularly enjoying this aspect of the subject.

Approaches taken to teaching students vary over the course of the junior cycle. While first year students are taught the basic knowledge and skills and classes involve mostly practical activities, classes in second and third year become more complicated and involve more theory as students are preparing for the Junior Certificate exam.

In general, students work on their own in the three subject classes. However, teachers encourage a certain amount of interaction with other students. There appears to be less of an emphasis on regular, formal homework in the technological subjects, although students are encouraged to revise class material on an on-going basis.

Chapter Eight

GENDER AND STUDENT PERFORMANCE IN THE TECHNOLOGICAL SUBJECTS

8.1 INTRODUCTION

The previous chapter described changes that have occurred in the syllabi of technological subjects and its implications for different groups of students. Recent syllabus changes were seen as making the technological subjects, at least potentially, more "girl-friendly". Furthermore, the more "hands-on" approach adopted in these classes accompanied by less of an emphasis on formal, written homework were seen as potential advantages in promoting engagement and achievement among students, both male and female, who are less academically oriented. This chapter is concerned with academic performance at junior cycle level exploring, specifically, the links between gender and performance within the three technological subjects. The effects of gender on academic achievement and performance have been well documented (Breen, 1986; Hannan et al., 1983; Hannan et al., 1996; Bahl and Woodhead, 1996) and continue to generate much attention and debate. However, little is known about performance patterns in specific subject areas such as technological subjects. This chapter addresses this gap in knowledge. The chapter starts out by discussing teachers' and fellow students' perceptions of girls' performance in the technological subjects. Section three presents the patterns of performance at Junior Certificate level while the fourth section concludes the chapter.

8.2 PERCEPTION OF GIRLS' PERFORMANCE
IN THE TECHNOLOGICAL SUBJECTS

In schools that provided some or all of the three technological subjects, teachers were asked about whether there were gender differences in classroom performance in their subject.

In general, teachers reported that there were few, if any, gender differences evident in overall performance levels with girls taking these subjects being as good as the boys:

> [Girls are] every bit as good [at Materials Technology], I'm not going to say they're better and most certainly not going to say they're worse, they're up there, (Oldham Way, high take-up in TG and MT, non-provision in MW, coed secondary)

> [Girls] would get on equally as well as the boys, if you had a group of girls that gelled together . . . (Clonmacken St., low take-up, community/comprehensive)

> They [girls] can [take the subject] because the work we would be doing wouldn't necessarily be very heavy work, it's skilful work and some are very good. . . . It seems to me I'll get out of a class, I'll get some very good girls and very good boys, it seems to be a fairly even mix. Are they generally better than the boys? I couldn't say they are, I'd say it would still work out about the same. (Churchwood, high take-up, vocational)

However, one teacher reported that girls tended to work more slowly in technological subject classes compared to boys, taking more time in preparing their projects:

> With the girls now at the moment in first year there has been a slight problem because they might be finished the project a little bit slower than the boys. (Riversdale Lane, low take-up, vocational)

Even though most teachers felt there was no difference in overall performance between male and female students, they reported that boys and girls brought different qualities to their work and these qualities were often described in highly gendered terms. In particular, girls' projects were described as "neater" and with a "better finish":

> Oh yeah, they [girls] mightn't have the physical strength for some things or at times I think they pretend they don't have . . . but in most cases the girls would present folders work better, they'll be that bit neater and they'll make a better effort at that so the few marks they may lose at one side, they'll gain it at the other side. (Longwell Green, high take-up, vocational)

> If the projects were displayed here you could walk around it and you could pick out, girl's project, girl's project, girl's project, absolutely no problem. Probably better finish, maybe not as technically challenging as what the boys might do but certainly better finish. (Clonmacken St., low take-up, community/comprehensive)

> I find girls are inclined to be neater. (Oldham Way, high take-up in TG and MT, non-provision in MW, coed secondary)

> I had girls there over the years and very good, they really fall into this thing of neatness and they love that presentation, very good presentation, whereas the boys don't, well some of the boys don't, but you can't even generalise like that because you get some boys there who would be very good that way. (Oldham Way, high take-up in TG and MT, non-provision in MW, coed secondary)

One teacher observed that having girls in the classroom enhances the performance of all students, in particular having a positive impact on the behaviour of boys in the class:

> I love a mix of girls and boys, for the class dynamic it's very good, if you have all girls and all boys, well it's a funny thing, in my subject the girls have a very civilising effect on bad language and different things, this has nothing to do with your subject but this will go across all the subjects. (Oldham Way, high take-up in TG and MT, non-provision in MW, coed secondary)

In general, subject teachers in Materials Technology (Wood), Metalwork and Technical Graphics considered that girls tended to perform about as well as boys in the practical classes. However, their performance was seen in somewhat gendered terms by teachers who emphasised stereo-typically feminine qualities such as neatness and precision.

Groups of second year boys in the case-study schools providing technological subjects were asked to describe how girls get on in technological subjects. A number of boys thought that girls performed equally well as boys in the technological subjects, sometimes even better:

> Boy: They [girls] have more patience than boys I'd say [in technological subjects]. (Male students, Clonmacken St., low take-up, community/comprehensive)
>
> Interviewer: So how do the girls get on with Woodwork?
>
> Boy: Pretty well, just the same.
>
> Interviewer: Do you think boys are better than girls?
>
> Boy: No, not really in all fairness.
>
> Interviewer: So you said that you have one girl in Technical Graphics?
>
> Boy: She's actually pretty good.
>
> Boy: She's the best...
>
> Boy: Yeah she's the best.
>
> Boy: She does everything, she's brilliant at it but you'll never hear from her, you hear from everybody else but she always gets everything done.
>
> Boy: I think [girls are] better at doing Tech Graphics because they're usually neater when they write. (Male students, Downend, low take-up, community/comprehensive)
>
> Boy: Yeah, the last year [she] was best in the class.
>
> Boy: She got an award.
>
> Boy: Yeah she got an award for [her work]. (Male students, Longwell Green, high take-up, vocational)

In Riversdale Lane school, however, the boys thought that girls are "possibly not" good at technological subjects as "boys are better with their hands" and "girls would be more into cooking and stuff". Misgivings about girls' performance were also expressed in Churchwood school. Physical strength was seen as a determinant of success in the subject:

> Interviewer: So do you think that the girls are better than boys in Metalwork?
>
> Boy: No.
>
> Boy: A good bit behind.
>
> . . .
>
> Interviewer: Why is that?
>
> Boy: We're quicker.
>
> Boy: Stronger.
>
> Boy: More strength.
>
> Boy: More strength yeah for filing and stuff.
>
> Boy: Cutting through it [metal].
>
> Boy: Bending and that.
>
> Interviewer: So you think that girls are not strong enough for Metalwork?
>
> Boy: Some of them.
>
> Boy: Some girls are.
>
> Boy: Some of them are too slow. (Male students, Churchwood, high take-up, vocational)

Girls were considered to be "alright" "but not as good" as boys at technological subjects by boys in Oldham way school.

In keeping with the gender stereotyping among students reported in Chapter Six, male students were more likely to report that taking technological subjects was not "appropriate" for girls mainly because they were unlikely to pursue related careers:

Interviewer: Why nationally do more boys than girls tend to do Woodwork, Metalwork and Technical Graphics?

Boy: Because they're more physical subjects, I suppose, you don't see many women architects and carpenters. (Male students, Downend, low take-up, community/comprehensive)

Boy: Girls aren't exactly going to get out and work on a building site and start cutting wood are they?

Boy: Girls should stick to their cooking. (Male students, Oldham Way, high take-up in TG and MT, coed secondary)

Stereotypes were also evident in relation to women in non-traditional occupations with some boys arguing that this pattern related to their lack of "physical strength" and interests (boys are "more into that stuff, more into cars . . ."):

Interviewer: Do you think that girls could have a career out of home, like in engineering?

Boy: You don't see many.

Boy: I doubt it.

Boy: You'd need to have physical strength and they wouldn't.

Boy: You don't need to have physical strength.

Boy: To be a mechanic you would. (Male students, Riversdale Lane, low take-up, vocational)

Boy: Because the girls do housework.

Boy: You'd hardly see girls welding.

Boy: And if the girls broke their nail...

Boy: Yeah ah my nail . . . roaring crying and all this.

Boy: You'd never see girls welding or anything like that. (Male students, Oakleaf Ave., low take-up, vocational)

In general, subject teachers reported that girls did as well as boys in the technological subjects, although some teachers characterised girls' approach in very stereotypically "feminine" terms, emphasising their neatness and application. Many boys in the case-study schools also felt that girls performed as well as boys in these subjects. However, some boys felt that male students were at an advantage in these subjects because of their physical strength and aptitude and because of the relevance of these subjects for their future careers.

8.3 SUBJECT LEVELS AND JUNIOR CERTIFICATE PERFORMANCE

It emerged from the interviews conducted with school personnel in the twelve schools that decisions as to whether students take subjects at higher or ordinary level were made at different stages within the junior cycle: either in the first, second or third year.

In some schools where streaming was practiced, there was a strong link between the class to which students were allocated and the level at which they took Junior Certificate subjects, including the technological subjects. Usually, higher streams tended to take subjects at higher level with the lowest stream likely to take ordinary level:

> By and large the bulk of the students in the top four streams would be doing honours and they would be working towards that from first year, and if there were a few that were struggling then maybe in third year they would decide that they might go for ordinary level. (Southmead, high take-up, community/comprehensive)

> In Metalwork, the top class would possible do honours, the middle class you'd be 50/50 and the lower class [would do ordinary]. (Glenveagh Road school, low take-up in TG and MT, medium take-up in MW)

In two other schools, teachers tended to orient students towards taking higher level in the exam. Taking this approach was seen by the Metalwork teacher in Churchwood school as motivating the less academically able students to keep up with the rest of the class:

> About Christmas in first year I would say to the students right we're doing higher level, you know with the class group that you have and now naturally we won't have 20 students of the very

same ability, you might have one or two who naturally will be a little bit weaker but if you set the standard for them the rest of the lads will be able to bring them along and the whole class can do higher level then or ordinary level, depending on the ability of the class. (Churchwood, high take-up, vocational)

Similarly, in Riversdale Lane school all students preparing for the Junior Certificate were expected to take Metalwork at higher level:

I have this rule for Junior Certs that every student does higher level, so when they come in in first year I would state this, that every student does higher level but that changes. Last year all students did higher level and I had a couple of very, very weak students but they got through it, they passed the higher level paper. Well I'll be honest with you, out of 44 [second years] I would safely say that 43 of them will be doing the higher level, 1 won't. (Riversdale Lane, low take-up, vocational)

However, less academically able students were seen as finding the higher level too difficult, according to a Technical Graphics Teacher in Churchwood school:

Even at this stage there's three or four of them [less academically able students] and they're under ferocious pressure, they're just not able but I'm not going to say anything to them, I'll just let them try the higher level and work their way through it, they'd be alright with the ordinary level and they'll know by Christmas if they're going to do it. (Churchwood, high take-up, vocational)

Only one teacher reported gender differences in the proportion of male and female students taking higher level in the technological subjects; he stressed that very few girls would take Technical Graphics at higher level in Junior Certificate, because of the perceived difficulty of the subject:

Very few of the girls would be taking honours, there's a little bit maybe association when it goes to the honours of Maths and it becomes a little bit mathematical, like you have to work out more stuff, a little bit abstract, you're given this and you have to work out, so it could be a little bit of geometry, maths geometry so they associate that, I don't know whether they associate it now, you can ask them that but it's about 60/40, 60 doing pass. (Oldham Way, high take-up in TG, and MT, non-provision in MW, coed secondary)

In sum, the case-study schools differ in the timing for selecting the subject level for the Junior Certificate as well as in the expectation that students would take technological subjects at higher level. Many teachers of technological subjects orient students towards the higher level in the subject they teach. In some schools, a link between streaming and the level of the subject was observed whereby higher stream classes take the subject at higher level. Only one teacher reported marked gender differences in the take-up of higher and ordinary level in the technological subjects.

Subject Levels and Junior Certificate Performance: The National Picture

An examination of the Junior Cycle examination database provided further information on the levels at which students took subjects along with their performance in Materials Technology (Wood), Metalwork and Technical Graphics. In 2003, the majority of students taking the technological subjects took these subjects at higher level; over two-thirds took Materials Technology (Wood) and Metalwork at higher level[12] but this was somewhat less common for those taking Technical Graphics with 56 per cent taking higher level[13] (see Figure 8.1). Among those taking the technological subjects, female students are less likely to take the subjects at higher level than their male counterparts. The gender difference is greater for Materials Technology and Metalwork than for Technical Graphics.

---

[12] This proportion taking higher level is comparable to a number of other Junior Certificate subjects, including Geography and German.

[13] This proportion is lower than for many other subjects, with the notable exceptions of Irish and Maths.

Figure 8.1: Proportion taking higher level by subject and gender

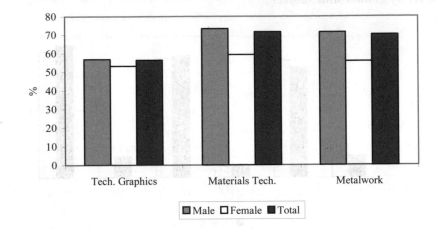

Male ☐ Female ■ Total

Source: Junior Certificate Examinations Database

Figure 8.2 presents the proportion of students who achieve A grades and A to C grades in the three subjects. Among students who take Technical Graphics at higher level, female students are slightly more likely than male students to achieve an A grade or a grade of C or above (Figure 8.2). The pattern is reversed for Materials Technology where male students do slightly better in terms of grades than female students. The greatest gender differences in performance are found in relation to Metalwork; 15 per cent of male students receive an A grade compared with 9 per cent of female students. These gender differences must be seen in the content of the lower average "ability" levels among girls taking Materials Technology (Wood) and Metalwork (see Chapter Three).

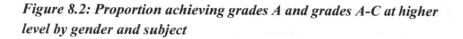

Figure 8.2: Proportion achieving grades A and grades A-C at higher level by gender and subject

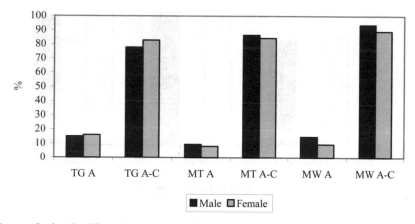

Source: Junior Certificate Examinations Database

Figure 8.3: Proportion achieving grades A and grades A-C at ordinary level by gender and subject

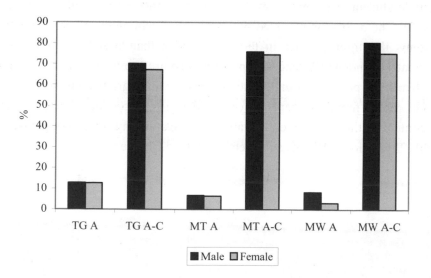

Source: Junior Certificate Examinations Database

Figure 8.3 provides information about students' exam performance at ordinary level. At ordinary level, male students achieve slightly higher grades (in terms of achieving a C grade or above) than female students across all three subjects, with the greatest difference found in relation to Metalwork.

As with subject take-up and choice, it is possible to use multilevel modelling to look at the school and student factors, which influence performance in these subjects. Table 8.1 presents the null model for each of the three subjects, that is, differences between schools and students before any characteristics are taken into account. Exam grades are scored from 0 (E, F or NG) to 7 (A on a higher level paper). The intercept indicates the average performance across all students in second-level schools. It is around a D grade on a higher-level paper for Technical Graphics and Materials Technology and close to a higher level C grade for Metalwork. The analyses indicate that schools account for almost a quarter of the variation in grades in Technical Graphics and Materials Technology and 31 per cent of the variation in Metalwork grades (Table 8.1). The amount of inter-school variation for Technical Graphics and Materials Technology performance is roughly comparable to that for English and Maths. The models also indicate the relationship between choice rates and performance at the school level. There is some evidence that schools with higher take-up rates in Technical Graphics tend to have lower average grades. No relationship between take-up and performance levels is evident for Materials Technology and Metalwork.

Table 8.1: Junior Cert exam performance — Null model

	Technical Graphics	**Materials Technology (Wood)**	**Metalwork**
Intercept	3.871	4.439	4.641
School-level variance	1.037*	0.842*	1.155*
Covariance with take-up	-0.264*	-0.008	-0.023
(correlation in parentheses)	(-0.307)	(-0.012)	(-0.027)
Student-level variance	3.156*	2.640*	2.531*
% variance at school level	24.7	24.2	31.3

Taking account of age and school characteristics, no significant gender differences in performance are evident (Table 8.2). Older students (that is, those aged over 16 years of age) tend to under-perform in exams relative to other students, a pattern that is consistent with previous research (see Hannan et al., 1996). Students in vocational schools tend to achieve lower grades in Technical Graphics than other students. This is likely to reflect differences between school sectors in the prior ability levels of students rather than differences in the "effects" of these schools per se (see Smyth, 1999). Girls in vocational and community/comprehensive schools tend to receive lower grades than their male counterparts in Technical Graphics. For Materials Technology, the lowest grades are found in vocational and boys' secondary schools while there is no significant variation in Metalwork grades by school sector. Students in larger schools receive higher grades in Technical Graphics but no such pattern is evident for the other two subjects. Students in designated disadvantaged schools tend to receive lower grades, reflecting student intake to these schools. Students in urban schools also receive lower grades, which is likely to reflect the socio-economic profile of these schools.

Student gender and age account for very little difference in student performance (1-3% of all variation across students). School and student characteristics account for between a quarter and a third of the initial differences between schools in their average grades.

In sum, male students are more likely than their female counterparts to take the technological subjects at higher level, with a more marked gender difference evident for Materials Technology (Wood) and Metalwork than for Technical Graphics. This difference must be seen in the context of the groups of students who select the subjects. Analyses in Chapter Three indicated tentative evidence that Materials Technology (Wood) and Metalwork tend to be taken by female students who achieve lower grades in their other Junior Certificate subjects; this pattern may account for gender differences in the proportion taking the subjects at higher level. In spite of these differences, analyses of a measure of Junior Certificate performance which combines level and grade into a single scale indicate no significant gender differences in performance in the three subjects.

Table 8.2: Factors predicting examination performance (Multilevel model)

	Technical Graphics	Materials Technology (Wood)	Metalwork
Intercept	4.162	5.371	5.465
Student characteristics			
Female	0.336	-0.249	-0.117
Age:			
15-15½	0.047	-0.008	0.128
15½-16	-0.066	-0.062	0.071
>16	-0.504*	-0.492*	-0.391*
(Contrast: <15)			
School characteristics			
School type:			
Boys' secondary	-0.014	-0.348*	-0.228
Girls' secondary	0.233	0.088	-
Vocational	-0.675*	-0.415*	-0.215
Comm./comp.	-0.206	-0.140	0.180
(Contrast: Coed sec.)			
Vocational*female	-0.354*	0.008	-0.468
Comm./comp.*female	-0.358*	-0.066	-0.348
School size:			
200-399	0.126	-0.177	-0.238
400-599	0.374*	-0.209	-0.351
600+	0.726*	-0.170	-0.191
(Contrast: <200)			
200-399*female	-0.313	-0.325	-0.627
400-599*female	-0.040	-0.186	0.058
600+*female	-0.234	-0.119	-0.193
Designated disadvantage	-0.555*	-0.389*	-0.507*
Disadvantaged*female	0.032	-0.077	0.156
Urban	-0.259*	-0.767*	-1.007*
Urban*female	0.071	0.160	0.238
School-level variance	0.695*	0.631*	0.853*
Covariance with take-up	-0.140*	0.029	0.043
(correlation in parentheses)	(-0.200)	(0.049)	(0.060)
Student-level variance	3.114*	2.586*	2.459*
% variance explained:			
School level	33.0	25.1	26.1
Student level	1.3	2.0	2.8

8.4 CONCLUSIONS

The chapter explored the perceptions of subject teachers and second year boys regarding girls' performance in practical classes. In general, teachers of technological subjects considered girls' performance to be as good as that of boys, although they often commented on female qualities such as neatness and precision. Several boys reported no gender differences in performance in the technological subjects although there were others who considered boys better at these subjects.

Investigation into the selection of subject levels revealed that there is considerable variation across the case-study schools in the timing of this process. While in some schools such a decision is made in first year, in others it is postponed until third year. A direct link between streaming and subject level taken could be identified whereby higher stream classes took the subjects at higher level.

An analysis of examination performance at the national level indicates a higher proportion of male students taking the subjects at higher level, a pattern that may be related to the prior academic ability levels of students taking the subjects. Controlling for age and school characteristics, no significant gender differences are found in the grades achieved within Materials Technology (Wood), Metalwork and Technical Graphics.

Chapter Nine

SUMMARY AND CONCLUSIONS

9.1 INTRODUCTION

The persistence of gender differentiation in subject choices within secondary and tertiary education in a number of countries has remained a subject for research interest and policy concern. In the Irish context, persistent gender differences are evident in second-level education, particularly in the take up of the technological subjects, Materials Technology (Wood), Metalwork and Technical Graphics. This pattern has potential implications for the skills acquired by young women, their engagement in education and for the education, training and labour market opportunities open to them on leaving school. This study set out to explore the factors shaping gender differences in the take-up of these traditionally "male" technological subjects at junior cycle level. This is a crucial stage in a student's schooling career as choices made at junior cycle have a significant impact on their subsequent educational pathways.

This study sets out to examine the role of school provision, school policy and student choice in shaping gender differences in the take-up of the technological subjects, namely Materials Technology (Wood), Metalwork and Technical Graphics. It draws on detailed case-studies in twelve second-level schools, case-studies based on interviews with key personnel (such as principals, guidance counsellors and teachers of the technological subjects) and with groups of students in each school. This allows us to document students' own experiences of selecting subjects at junior cycle level, placing their accounts within the context of school policy and practice. The following section presents the main findings of the study while section three discusses the implications of these findings for policy development regarding gender equity in subject take-up.

9.2 SUMMARY OF THE MAIN FINDINGS

Subject provision

Materials Technology (Wood) and Technical Graphics are provided in the majority of second-level schools while Metalwork is provided in only four out of ten schools. Whether the technological subjects are provided in a school is strongly related to school characteristics, such as school type, size, disadvantaged status and location. In other words, student access to these technological subjects depends on the school they attend.

The three technological subjects are more commonly provided in the vocational and community/comprehensive sectors, reflecting, on the one hand, the historical tradition of an applied orientation within vocational schools and, on the other hand, the emphasis within the community/comprehensive sector on bridging the gap between secondary and vocational schools by providing a broad curriculum for students. In contrast, only a very small number of girls' secondary schools provide any of the technological subjects with no girls' school providing Metalwork. This too must be seen in historical context, as girls' schools were traditionally more likely to provide humanities and "accomplishment" subjects (such as Music and Art) (see Hannan et al., 1983).

Over and above the effect of school sector, larger schools are significantly more likely to provide the three technological subjects than smaller schools, all else being equal. This is in keeping with previous research (see, for example, Smyth et al., 2004), which indicates that larger schools tend to provide a broader curriculum to their students while smaller schools are subject to logistical and resource constraints in so doing. Designated disadvantaged schools are significantly more likely to provide Materials Technology (Wood) and Metalwork than other schools while urban schools (that is, those in Dublin, Cork, Limerick, Waterford and Galway cities) are less likely to provide the technological subjects.

The subjects provided within a school, therefore, reflect historical tradition along with assumptions about the suitability of certain subjects for their student population. Thus, the technological subjects have traditionally been seen as more suitable for boys, especially those from working-class backgrounds. In addition, patterns of subject provision point towards resource and size constraints among smaller schools.

Subject take-up

Research carried out in Ireland and internationally points to a range of influences at the individual and school level on subject choice (see Chapter 1). In terms of individual factors, students are likely to take subjects they are interested in, ones they perceive as useful for the future and ones in which they expect to perform well. However, students make decisions within a specific school context and their choices are therefore likely to be influenced by school structures and practices (for example, the options available and how they are packaged) as well as the social context in terms of their teachers and peers.

As a result, the provision patterns highlighted in the previous section are not the only factor shaping subject take-up. Exploring take-up of the three technological subjects, it was found that the proportion of students taking these subjects varied significantly across different kinds of schools. Among schools providing technological subjects, take-up of these subjects is higher in smaller schools and schools in rural locations, all else being equal. The pattern for smaller schools is most likely related to the more constrained curriculum in these schools; if students have fewer choices in a school providing technological subjects, then they are more likely to take these subjects. Furthermore, take-up of Materials Technology (Wood) and Metalwork is higher in designated disadvantaged schools, most likely reflecting the fact that students come from working-class backgrounds and may perceive these subjects as more useful in terms of accessing skilled manual work in the future. All else being equal, students in the vocational sector are more likely to take at least one of the technological subjects than those in other school types.

Gender differences in take-up persist even within schools providing the subjects (see Hannan et al., 1983). If only students attending schools that provide the subject are considered, 11 per cent of female students took Technical Graphics compared with 46 per cent of males in schools providing the subject; 15 per cent of female students took Materials Technology (Wood) compared with 59 per cent of males; and 7 per cent of female students took Metalwork compared with 51 per cent of male students. Interestingly, however, the gender gap in take-up is somewhat narrower in larger schools and schools located in urban areas. Provision patterns for the technological subjects therefore account for only some of the gender difference in take-up patterns. The other factors shaping these take-up differences are discussed in the remainder of this section.

The choice process within schools

As is the case for second-level schools nationally, the case-study schools were found to differ in the timing of subject choice for junior cycle subjects and in the degree of choice allowed to students. Some of the case-study schools required students to select their subjects before entry to the school while others allowed students to "sample" subjects for part of first year before making their selection. These differences in the timing of subject choice meant that schools varied in the nature and timing of information given to students regarding the different subjects on offer. In schools with a taster programme where students sampled subjects for part of first year, exposure to the subject was seen as allowing students to make a more informed choice based on their interests and abilities. In other schools, information on subject options was provided as part of an open day or evening for students and their parents or, in some cases, through contact between the second-level school and the primary school (in the form of visits and induction days).

The school's approach to the timing of subject choice meant that students had different levels of knowledge about what was involved in taking a particular subject. For those in schools with a taster programme, they had greater insight into the content of the subject. In contrast, students in the case-study schools where they were required to select their subject before or on entry to the school were more reliant on informal sources of advice such as family or friends, although it should be noted that all students relied on parents as a source of advice and information (see below). It could be argued that, if parents and friends have no detailed and up-to-date knowledge of the content of the technological subjects and/or have more stereotyped perceptions of them as "boys' subjects", then this will have consequences for the choices made by students and the reproduction of gender stereotypes. Such gender stereotyping has received a good deal of attention in international research with a number of studies highlighting the impact of early socialisation on what constitutes "appropriate" jobs for men and women (Helwig, 1998; Miller and Budd, 1999).

On the basis of the patterns in the case-study schools, there appears to be no clear relationship between the timing of subject choice and whether female students have a higher take-up of the technological subjects. What did distinguish between the "high take-up" and the "low take-up" schools was the way in which subject choices were structured. Among the "high take-up" schools, two patterns were evident. In two of the schools (Longwell Green and Churchwood), all students, both male and female, were required to take Materials Technology (Wood); furthermore, in Southmead school, all students in the lower stream class were required to take Metalwork. The other pattern was one of "constrained choice": in Oldham Way, students were required to select two subjects out of Materials Technology (Wood), Metalwork and Home Economics, thus requiring female students to take at least one traditionally male practical subject. In contrast, in the "low take-up" schools, students were required to select technological subjects from a wider range of subjects. In some cases, option packages were such that students were required to directly choose between a traditionally male and a traditionally female subject; thus, in Glenveagh Road, students were required to select between Home Economics and Materials Technology (Wood). While such packaging of subjects may be designed to facilitate student demand, it is also likely to reinforce gender differentiation in subject take-up. The lower take-up of technological subjects among female students must be seen as reflecting, at least in part, the school's approach to allocating subjects to certain groups of students and to the way in which the schools "package" subject options through timetabling practices.

Factors shaping subject choice

Schools structure subject choice among students as their choices are, to some extent, "constrained". A number of students in the case-study schools were dissatisfied with these constraints on their choices while students in five of the schools were not always allocated the subjects they selected due to certain subjects being over-subscribed. It is important to recognise, however, that many students are themselves actively involved in the choice process. Students in the case-study schools were asked about the sources of advice they drew on in making their decisions and the factors that most influenced their choice of subjects at junior cycle level. Parents were the most commonly mentioned influence on students' decision-making, in line with other international research (see, for example, Stables, 1996). However, there was no evidence that parents generally actively discouraged (or encouraged) girls' selecting any of the three technological subjects.[1] Other sources of informal advice included older siblings and friends.

A number of students selected subjects because of an underlying interest in the subject or because they felt they would do well in the subject, in keeping with previous international research (see Eccles, 1994). In selecting the technological subjects, students (male and female alike) were often motivated by wanting a "break" from more academic subjects, by a greater hands-on emphasis in these subjects and by the more informal class atmosphere (with students allowed to move around and talk to other students). This is consistent with other international research which indicates that both boys and girls are attracted to technology education because they enjoy working with their hands and like the opportunity for independence and creativity afforded by these classes (see Silverman and Pritchard, 1996). Students in case-study schools with a taster programme were more likely to mention their perceptions of the subject and the teacher as a reason for selecting (or dropping) a particular subject, although students across all schools were highly reliant on their parents' advice, even though they sometimes chose to ignore it.

Students' reliance on informal sources of information, such as parents, siblings and friends, is likely to have implications for the kinds of subjects they select. Parents may rely on their own schooling experiences in giving advice to their children but may not have taken particular subjects or may not be aware of changes in the subject content and assess-

---

[1] However, in a number of cases parents recommended Business Studies over other subjects as being "useful for the future".

ment approach since their own schooldays. This highlights the importance of providing comprehensive information on the nature of subjects to students and their parents before they choose subjects.

Gender stereotyping in second-level subjects

Strong gender stereotyping was evident in student attitudes to the technological subjects in the case-study schools. Many students, both male and female, saw gender differences in take-up of these subjects as reflecting underlying differences in interest in particular subjects with a view that "girls don't really like doing boys' subjects". The perception of the technological subjects, most notably Metalwork, as "dirty", "noisy" and requiring physical strength meant that many students felt that these subjects were more appropriate for male students. This contrasts with the feeling among subject teachers that syllabus changes (especially in Materials Technology (Wood) and Metalwork), resulting in a shift away from a skills-based focus to an emphasis on design, have made the subjects, at least potentially, more "girl-friendly". The labelling of the technological subjects as "male" by many students was also linked to gender stereotypes in related occupational areas; thus, girls were seen as less likely to take these subjects because they were unlikely to pursue a career in a related trade (such as mechanic or plumber). Furthermore, existing gender differences in take-up could become self-perpetuating in schools as female students were reluctant to be "pioneers", that is, to be the only girl in a class of boys.

Although gender stereotyping among students was quite strong within the case-study schools, some students, both female and male, did actively challenge this labelling and viewed the subjects as appropriate for all students. In addition, even among students with gendered views, there were contradictions in students' perceptions. Some boys had "no problem" with girls taking technological subjects but highlighted "natural" male superiority in these subjects. Some female students felt that all students should have access to these subjects but would not themselves want to select such subjects. Although a number of female students did report being jeered by male students within technological subject classes and a couple of student groups reported stereotyped views among some teachers (see also Gillborn, 1990), the perceptions of the subjects as "male" seemed to have a much stronger influence on students' decision-making than active dissuasion by teachers or male students.

9.3 IMPLICATIONS FOR POLICY DEVELOPMENT

The findings of this study raise a number of issues for policy development regarding gender equity in subject take-up. These issues centre on provision patterns, the timing of subject choice, the availability of information on subject content, timetabling practices and the challenging of gender stereotypes. A number of the recommendations relate to policy and practice at the national level, proposing action on the part of the Department of Education and Science and other statutory bodies such as the National Council for Curriculum and Assessment (NCCA). However, it is important to recognise that "schools can make a difference", that is, that policy and practice at the school level can be used to promote equal opportunities in subject take-up.

Currently, provision patterns mean that many students, especially girls, attend schools where the technological subjects are not provided. These patterns reflect, at least in part, assumptions about student demand for particular kinds of subjects along with resource constraints (relating to both facilities and teacher availability). In particular, girls' secondary schools are extremely unlikely to provide any of the three technological subjects. The Physics-Chemistry Intervention Project (Ní Chárthaigh and O'Brien, 1996) may provide a model for exploring the possibility of extending provision of the technological subjects by providing support and resources for schools which do not currently have these subjects. However, the resource requirements are likely to be substantial and expanding provision without complementary measures to change student attitudes (see below) is unlikely to be effective in reducing gender differences in take-up.

Second-level schools in Ireland vary considerably in the timing of subject choice and the degree of subject choice afforded to students. Previous research has shown that postponing subject choice until students have had a chance to try out the different subjects is favoured by students and has a neutral, if not positive, effect on academic performance

(Smyth, 1999; Smyth et al., 2004). Having a taster programme will also mean that female students have at least some exposure to traditionally male subjects (and male students to traditionally female subjects). Providing a taster programme, however, has significant resource implications for schools and may be even more difficult for smaller schools with a constrained curriculum. It is recommended, therefore, that schools should be encouraged to introduce a taster programme in their school and that the appropriate resources be allocated to schools to maximise student options.

Students' reliance on informal sources of advice in making their decisions along with the requirement in many schools for students to select their subject before entry mean that the provision of accurate information to students and their parents on the different subject options is crucial. However, at present formal guidance provision for junior cycle students is relatively scant (see McCoy et al., forthcoming), a pattern that is especially problematic given the strong influence of decisions made at junior cycle level on choices right up to higher education entry (see Smyth, Hannan, 2002). It is recommended, therefore, that schools should aim to provide students and their parents with clear and comprehensive information on (changes in) the content of particular subjects and on the links between junior cycle subjects and senior cycle subjects, education/training courses and relevant occupational opportunities (including newer occupational niches). They should aim, in so doing, to discourage gender stereotypes in subject selection, perhaps by drawing on examples of female role models in "male" occupations. This effort at the school level could be facilitated by the development and design of user-friendly material by the Department of Education and Science in conjunction with the NCCA on the different subject areas for dissemination to parents and students making the transition to second-level education.

The way in which subjects are offered to students has a strong influence on patterns of take-up. Schools should, therefore, aim to avoid timetabling subjects in such a way that students must directly select between traditionally male and traditionally female subjects. In cases where places in a particular subject are limited and courses oversubscribed, places should be allocated in an equitable way between male and female students.

Changes in provision patterns, information provision and timetabling practices will go some way towards facilitating gender equity in subject take-up. However, the main barrier remains strongly stereotyped perceptions among students of subjects as "male" or "female". It is recommended that courses such as Social, Personal and Health Education and Civic, Social and Political Education should increase their emphasis on addressing issues around gender equity with students in order to challenge stereotypical views. The provision of information which indicates the relevance of the technological subjects to a wide range of skills and career options (see above) should also be helpful in this regard. However, it should be acknowledged that intervention to promote gender equity in subject take-up may have a limited effect; interventions in the British context have indicated that they may alter students' attitudes to some extent but not necessarily their behaviour in terms of subject and occupational choice (see Kelly, 1988).

In conclusion, there is a strong case for promoting greater gender equity in the take-up of the technological subjects. Firstly, these subjects contribute to the development of manipulative and design skills which are useful for a range of different career options for young women and men as well as contributing to their more general life-skills. Secondly, a balance between more hands-on activities and more "academic" subjects appears to promote student engagement in schoolwork, especially for less academically oriented young people, and is therefore likely to have a longer-term influence on their retention and achievement within the educational system. Thirdly, lack of access to the technological subjects may close off certain education and career options for female students, not just in terms of skilled craft work but in terms of professions such as engineering and architecture. It is hoped that this study has highlighted elements of policy and practice which could move the situation beyond the view of technological subjects as "boys' subjects".

REFERENCES

Ayalon, H. (1995). "Math as a Gatekeeper: Ethnic and Gender Inequality in Course-taking of the Sciences in Israel", *American Journal of Education*, Vol. 104, pp. 34-56.

Bahl, Kamlesh and Woodhead, Chris (1996). *The Gender Divide: Performance Differences between Boys and Girls at School*. London: HMSO.

Bandura, Albert, Barbaranelli, Claudio, Caprara, Gian Vittorio and Pastorelli, Concetta (2001). "Self-Efficacy Beliefs as Shapers of Children's Aspirations and Career Trajectories", *Child Development*, Vol. 72, No. 1, pp. 187-206.

Barnes, G., McInerney, D. and H.W. Marsh (1999). "The Science Enrolment Model: An Expectancy/Value Model of Enrolment Behaviour in Elective Science Courses", Presentation to the European Conference on Educational Research, Lahti.

Blackwell, L. (2001) "Occupational sex segregation and part-time work in modern Britain", *Gender, Work and Organization*, Vol. 8, pp. 146-163.

Bradley, Harriet (1989). *Men's Work, Women's Work: A Sociological History of the Sexual Division of Labour in Employment*. Cambridge: Polity Press.

Breen, Richard (1986). *Subject Availability and Student Performance in the Senior Cycle of Irish Post-primary Schools*. General Research Series no. 129, Dublin: Economic and Social Research Institute.

Buchmann, M. and Charles, M. (1995). "Organizational and institutional factors in the process of gender stratification: comparing social arrangements in six European countries", *International Journal of Sociology*, Vol. 25, pp. 66-95.

Ciccocioppo, Anna-Lisa, Stewin, Leonard L., Madill, Helen M., Montgomerie, T. Craig, Tovell, Dorothy R., Armour, Margaret-Ann and Fitzsimmons, George W. (2002). "Transitional Patterns of Adolescent Females in Non-traditional Career Paths", *Canadian Journal of Counselling*, Vol. 36, No. 1, pp. 25-37.

Cockburn, Cynthia (1983). *Brothers: Male Dominance and Technological Change*. London: Pluto Press.

Cockburn, Cynthia (1987). *Two Track Training: Sex Inequalities and the YTS.* Basingstoke: Macmillan.

Cullen, Mary (1987). *Girls Don't Do Honours: Irish Women in Education in the 19th and 20th Centuries.* Dublin: Women's Education Bureau.

Dale, Angela, Jackson, Nors and Hill, Nicky (2005). *Women in Non-traditional Training and Employment.* Manchester: Equal Opportunities Commission.

Daly, P. and Shuttleworth, I. (1997). "Determinants of Public Examination Entry and Attainment in Mathematics: Evidence on gender and gender-type of school from the 1980s and 1990s in Northern Ireland", *Evaluation and Research in Education*, Vol. 11, No. 2, pp. 91-101.

Davies, Peter, Telhaj, Shqiponje, Hutton , David, Adnett, Nick and Coe, Robert (2004a). "Institutional and social background effects on the probability of taking an examination subject at age 16", Paper presented at British Educational Research Association Conference UMIST, Manchester.

Davies, Peter, Telhaj, Shqiponje, Hutton, David, Adnett, Nick and Coe, Robert (2004b). "The Myth of the Bog Standard Secondary School: a school level analysis of students' choice of optional subjects", Paper prepared for BERA 2004, Manchester.

Department of Education and Science (various years). *Statistical Report.* Dublin: Stationery Office.

Ditchburn, G. and Martin, J. (1986). *Education for Girls in Catholic and Independent Schools in the Western Suburbs of Melbourne and Gippsland.* Non-government Schools Participation and Equity Project, Victoria.

Dryler, H. (1999). "The impact of school and classroom characteristics on educational choices by boys and girls: a multilevel analysis", *Acta Sociologica*, Vol. 42, pp. 299-318.

Eccles, Jacquelynne S. (1994). "Understanding Women's Educational and Occupational Choices. Applying the Eccles et al. Model of Achievement-Related Choices", *Psychology of Women Quarterly*, Vol. 18, No. 4, pp. 585-609.

Epstein, D., Elwood, J., Hey, V. and Maw, J. (eds.) (1998). *Failing Boys? Issues in Gender and Achievement.* Buckingham: Open University Press.

ETAN Expert Working Group on Women and Science (2000). *Science Policies in the European Union: Promoting Excellence through Mainstreaming Gender Equality.* Brussels: European Commission.

Evetts, Julia (1993). "Women in Engineering: educational concomitants of a non-tradiational career choice", *Gender and Education*, Vol. 5, No. 2, pp.167-178.

Finn, Jeremy D. (1998). "Taking Foreign Languages in High School", *Foreign Language Annals*, Vol. 31, No. 3, pp. 287-306.

Francis, Becky (2002). "Is the Future Really Female? The Impact and Implications of Gender for 14-16 Year Olds' Career Choices", *Journal of Education and Work*, Vol. 15, No. 1, pp. 75-88.

Gash, H., Morgan, M., and Sugrue, C. (1993). "Effects of an intervention and school type on gender stereotypes", *Irish Journal of Education*, Vol. 27, pp. 60-70.

Gaskell, Jane (1984). "Gender and Course Choice: The Orientation of Male and Female Students", *Journal of Education*, Vol. 166, No. 1, pp.89-102.

Gillborn, David (1990). "Sexism and Curricular 'Choice'", *Cambridge Journal of Education*, Vol. 20, No. 2, pp. 161-174.

Gorard, Stephen and Taylor, Chris (2004). *Combining Methods in Educational and Social Research*. Berkshire: Open University Press.

Greene, Cherry K. and Stitt-Gohdes, Wanda L. (1997). "Factors That Influence Women's Choices to Work in the Trades", *Journal of Career Development*, Vol. 23, No. 4, pp. 265-278.

Hannan, D. F., Breen, R., Murray, B., Watson, D., Hardiman, N. and O'Higgins, K. (1983). *Schooling and Sex Roles*. Dublin: The Economic and Social Research Institute.

Hannan, D.F., McCabe, B. and McCoy, S. (1998). *Trading Qualifications for Jobs: Overeducation and the Irish Youth Labour Market*. Dublin: The Economic and Social Research Institute.

Hannan, Damian F., Ó Riain, Sean (1993). *Pathways to Adulthood: Causes and Consequences of Success and Failure in Transitions amongst Irish Youth*. Dublin: The Economic and Social Research Institute.

Hannan, D.F. and Shortall, S. (1991). *The Quality of their Education: School Leavers' Views of Educational Objectives and Outcomes*. Dublin: The Economic and Social Research Institute.

Hannan, D.F., Smyth, E., McCullagh, J., O'Leary, R., McMahon, D. (1996). *Coeducation and Gender Equality*, Dublin: Oak Tree Press/ Economic and Social Research Institute.

Harris, M. 1979. *Cultural Materialism: the Struggle for a Science of Culture*. Random House, New York

Helwig, Andrew A. (1998). "Gender-Role Stereotyping: Testing Theory with a Longitudinal Sample", *Sex Roles*, Vol. 38, No. 5/6, pp. 403-423.

Henwood, Flis (1998). "Engineering Difference: discourses on gender, sexuality and work in a college of technology", *Gender and Education*, Vol. 10, No. 1, pp.35-49.

Johnson, R. Burke and Onwuegbuzie, Anthony J. (2004). "Mixed methods research: a paradigm whose time has come", *Educational Researcher*, Vol. 33, No. 7, pp.14-26.

Jonsson, J.O. (1999). "Explaining sex differences in educational choice: an empirical assessment of a rational choice model", *European Sociological Review*, Vol. 15, No. 4, pp. 391-404.

Kelly, Alison (1981). *The Missing Half: Girls and Science Education*. Manchester: Manchester University Press.

Kelly, Alison (1985). "The construction of masculine science", *British Journal of Sociology of Education*, Vol. 6, No. 2, pp. 133-154.

Kelly, Alison (1988). "Option Choice for Girls and Boys", *Research in Science and Technological Education*, Vol. 6, No. 1, pp. 5-23.

Kitchen, A. (1999). "The changing profile of entrants to mathematics at A level and to mathematical subjects in higher education", *British Educational Research Journal*, Vol. 25, No. 1, pp. 57-74.

Laursen, Per F. (1993). "Students' Choice and Social Selection", *Scandinavian Journal of Educational Research*, Vol. 37, No. 4, pp. 279-291.

Lee, V. and Smith, J. (1993). "Effects of School Restructuring on the Achievement and Engagment of Middle-Grade Students", *Sociology of Education*, Vol. 66, pp. 164-187.

Manthorpe, C.A. (1982). "Men's science, women's science or science? Some issues related to the study of girls' science education", *Studies in Science Education*, Vol. 9, pp. 65-80.

Marsh, Herbert W. and Yeung, Alexander Seeshing (1997). "Coursework Selection: Relations to Academic Self-Concept and Achievement", *American Educational Research Journal*, Vol. 34, No. 4, pp. 691-720.

McCoy, Selina, Smyth, Emer, Darmody, Merike and Dunne, Allison (forthcoming). *Guidance for All? Guidance Provision in Second-level Schools*. Dublin: ESRI.

McKinnon, Margaret and Ahola-Sidaway, Janice (1995). "'Workin' with the Boys': a North American perspective on non-traditional work initiatives for adolescent females in secondary schools", *Gender and Education*, Vol. 7, No. 3, pp.327-339.

Millar, David and Kelly, Donal (1999). *From Junior to Leaving Certificate: A Longitudinal Study of 1994 Junior Certificate Candidates who took the Leaving Certificate Examination in 1997*. Dublin: NCCA/ERC.

Miller, Linda and Budd, Jacqueline (1999). "The Development of Occupational Sex-role Stereotypes, Occupational Preferences and Academic Subject Preferences in Children at Ages 8, 12 and 16", *Educational Psychology*, Vol. 19, No. 1, pp. 17-35.

Nash, Melanie, Allsop, Terry and Woolnough, Brian (1984). "Factors Affecting Pupil Uptake of Technology at 14+", *Research in Science and Technological Education*, Vol. 2, No. 1, pp. 5-19.

NCCA (1999). *The Junior Cycle Review. Progress Report: Issues and Options for Development*. Dublin: NCCA.

NCCA (2004). *Board of Studies for the Review of Technological Education in the Junior Cycle: Final Report*. Dublin: NCCA.

Ní Chárthaigh, D. and O'Brien, J. (1996). *Department of Education Intervention Projects in Physics and Chemistry*. Limerick: Centre for Studies in Gender and Education, University of Limerick.

Oakes, J. (1990). *Multiplying Inequalities: The Effects of Race, Social Class and Tracking on Opportunities to Learn Mathematics and Science*. California: Rand.

Oakes, J., Selvin, M., Karoly, L., and G. Guiton (1992). *Educational Matchmaking: Academic and Vocational Tracking in Comprehensive High Schools*. California: Rand.

Raftery, Deirdre (2001). "The Academic Formation of the Fin de Siecle Female: Schooling for Girls in Late Nineteenth Century Ireland", *Irish Educational Studies*, Vol. 20, pp. 321-334.

Read, Barbara K. (1994). "Motivational Factors in Technical College Women's Selection of Nontraditional Careers", *Journal of Career Development*, Vol. 20, No. 3, pp. 239-258.

Riddell, Sheila (1992). *Gender and the Politics of the Curriculum*. London: Routledge.

Rubery, J. and Fagan, C. (1995). "Gender segregation in societal context", *Work, Employment and Society*, Vol. 9, pp. 213-240.

Sammons, P., Thomas, S. and Mortimore, P. (1997). *Forging Links: Effective Schools and Effective Departments*. London: Paul Chapman.

Scott, A.M. (ed.)(1994). *Gender Segregation and Social Change*. Oxford: Oxford University Press.

Sexton, J.J., Hughes, G. and Finn, C. (2002). *Occupational Employment Forecasts 2015*. Dublin: FÁS/ESRI.

Shuttleworth, I. and Daly, P. (1997). "Inequalities in the uptake of science at GCSE: evidence from Northern Ireland", *Research Papers in Education*, Vol. 12, No. 2, pp. 143-156.

Silverman, Suzanne and Alice M. Pritchard (1996). "Building Their Future: Girls and Technology Education in Connecticut", *Journal of Technology Education*, Vol. 7, No. 2, Spring, pp. 41-54.

Smyth, Emer (1999) *Do Schools Differ? Academic and Personal Development among Pupils in the Second-Level Sector*. Dublin: Oak Tree Press/ESRI.

Smyth, Emer (2002). "Gender differentiation and early labour market integration across Europe", in Irena Kogan and Walter Müller (eds.), *School-to-Work Transitions in Europe: Analyses of the EULFS 2002 Ad Hoc Module*. Mannheim: MZES.

Smyth, Emer and Hannan, Carmel (2002). *Who Chooses Science? Subject Choice in Second-level Schools*. Dublin: Liffey Press/ESRI.

Smyth, Emer, McCoy, Selina and Darmody, Merike (2004). *Moving Up: The Experiences of First Year Students in Post-primary Education*. Dublin: Liffey Press/ESRI.

Spade, J.Z., Columba, L. and B.E. Vanfossen (1997). "Tracking in mathematics and science: course and course-selection procedures", *Sociology of Education*, Vol. 70, No. 2, pp. 108-127.

Spender, Dale (1980). *Learning to Lose: Sexism and Education*. London: Women's Press.

Stables, Andrew (1990). "Differences between pupils from mixed and single sex schools in their enjoyment of school subjects and in their attitudes to sciences and to school", *Education Review*, Vol. 42, No. 93, pp. 221-230.

Stables, Andrew (1996). *Subjects of Choice: The Process and Management of Pupil and Student Choice*. London: Cassell.

Stables, Andrew and Stables, Sian (1995). "Gender differences in students' approaches to A-level subject choices and perceptions of A-level subjects: a study of first-year A-level students in a tertiary college", *Educational Research*, Vol. 37, No. 1, pp. 39-51.

Stokking, K.M. (2000). "Predicting the choice of physics in secondary education", *International Journal of Science Education*, Vol. 22, No. 12, pp. 1261-1283.

Tashakorri, A. and Teddlie, C. (eds.)(2002). *Handbook of Mixed Methods in Social and Behavioral Research*. California: Sage.

Thurtle, Val, Hammond, Shaun and Paul Jennings (1998). "The Experience of Students in a Gender Minority on Courses at a College of Higher and Further Education", *Journal of Vocational Education and Training*, Vol. 50, No. 4, pp. 629-646.

Whitehead, J.A. (1996). "Sex stereotypes, gender identity and subject choice at A-level", *Educational Research,* Vol. 2 (Summer), pp. 147-160.